DATE DUE

THE PRIMA DONNA

Da Capo Press Music Reprint Series

MUSIC EDITOR

BEA FRIEDLAND
Ph.D., City University of New York

This title was recommended for Da Capo reprint by
Frank D'Accone, *University of California at Los Angeles*

THE PRIMA DONNA

Her History and Surroundings from the Seventeenth to
the Nineteenth Century

BY

H. SUTHERLAND EDWARDS

IN TWO VOLUMES

VOL. II

DA CAPO PRESS • NEW YORK • 1978

Library of Congress Cataloging in Publication Data

Edwards, Henry Sutherland, 1828-1906.
   The prima donna.

   (Da Capo Press music reprint series)
   Reprint of the 1888 ed. published by Remington, London.
   1. Singers—Biography. 2. Opera. I. Title.
ML400.E28 1978   782.1'092'2 [B]   77-17875
ISBN 0-306-77536-0

This Da Capo Press edition of *The Prima Donna, Volume II*
is an unabridged republication of the first edition
published in London in 1888.

Published by Da Capo Press, Inc.
A Subsidiary of Plenum Publishing Corporation
227 West 17th Street, New York, N.Y. 10011

THE PRIMA DONNA

THE PRIMA DONNA

Her History and Surroundings from the Seventeenth to
the Nineteenth Century

BY

H SUTHERLAND EDWARDS

IN TWO VOLUMES

VOL II

London
REMINGTON AND CO PUBLISHERS
HENRIETTA STREET COVENT GARDEN
1888

Preposterous ass! that never read so far
To know the cause why music was ordained!
Was it not to refresh the mind of man
After his studies or his usual pain?

Taming of the Shrew.

Shining ones who thronged
Eastward and westward making bright the night.

Light of Asia.

Soprano, mezzo, even the contralto
Wished him five fathoms under the Rialto.

Beppo.

CONTENTS.

CHAPTER I.

JENNY LIND.

MADAME LIND-GOLDSCHMIDT was one of the few perfect
singers of the century; though so many years have
passed since she appeared on the operatic stage that
this statement must, by most amateurs of the present
day, be taken on trust. She filled her last operatic
part at the end of the season of 1848. It is true
that, for many years afterwards, she was heard from
time to time at concerts, even down to the year
1866. But the Jenny Lind who touched the hearts
and turned the heads of all who heard her may be
said to have disappeared in little more than a year
from the day when, in the spring of 1847, she first
came before the London public. No great singer
had ever a shorter career, or a career that was more
brilliant. Born at Stockholm on 6th Oct., 1820 (or,

according to some chroniclers, 1821), Jenny Lind
sang before she was able to speak. She was the
daughter of educated parents, the father being a
teacher of languages, the mother a schoolmistress.
Little Jenny sang every air she happened to hear,
and did so without attracting much attention until
one day her lisping performances were heard by an
actress named Landberg, who, struck by the child's
musical genius, urged the parents to give her a
serious artistic training. They disliked the idea of
their child devoting herself to the stage, but with
their consent Frau Landberg spoke to Jenny herself
on the subject, and the result was that the young
girl was introduced to a well-known music-master
in Stockholm, who, after hearing her sing, predicted for her a most brilliant future. After
giving her some lessons, Jenny's master presented
her to Count Pücke, director of the Court Theatre,
with the view of getting her admitted to the School
of Music, which, like the theatre connected with it,
was under the Count's direction. But the little
girl made no favourable impression on the Inten-
dant, and it was not until after many representations that he could be induced to accept her.

Her teachers, when she had once passed the ordeal
of the Count's criticism, were Berg, principal singing-master of the school, and the composer Lindblad.
Attached to the School of Music was a small theatre

for students; and there, when scarcely in her teens,
Jenny Lind appeared in child's parts with considerable success. Soon afterwards, at the critical
period of from thirteen to fourteen, the voice of the
little girl became clouded, and she seemed to have
lost her upper notes. For a time she gave up singing altogether; but, far from abandoning her musical
studies, she pursued them in a new direction, and
for some two or three years occupied herself chiefly
with harmony and the practice of the pianoforte.
Then the voice returned, and one night when the
fourth act of *Robert le Diable* was to be performed,
or at least sung, at a concert, Jenny Lind had the
part of "Alice" offered to her. She sang the
beautiful air "Quand je quittais la Normandie"
with so much expression and so much charm that
everyone, even her own singing - master, was
astonished. Jenny, too, was herself a little surprised when, the next morning, she was told that she
was now to appear on the boards, and that she had
already been cast for the part of "Agatha" in *Der
Freischütz.* Fortunately she had studied the music,
and there was no character which she was more
desirous of impersonating. Her success was already
looked upon as certain when, to the admiration of
all present, she sang the part at the last rehearsal.
Among the audience at the representation was the
famous and fascinating novelist, Frederika Bremer,

who has described Jenny Lind's first appearance in
enthusiastic terms.

Jenny Lind was now the accepted favourite of
Stockholm opera-goers; and for nearly two years
afterwards she sang on the scene of her first appearance the principal soprano parts in Weber's
Euryanthe, in Meyerbeer's *Robert le Diable*, and in
Spontini's *Vestale*. Her first Italian part was
"Anna Bolena" in Donizetti's opera of that name,
considered, in the days before *Lucia*, *Lucrezia Borgia*,
and *La Favorita*, the composer's master-piece.
But it was not in Italian works that the young
Swedish singer was to make her greatest success;
and in the year 1840 the eyes of most ambitious
vocalists, as of musicians generally, were turned
towards Paris. "This city," wrote Heine, about
the year 1840, or a few years later, "is not simply
the capital of France, but of the whole civilized
world, and the meeting-place of its intellectual
notabilities. Assembled here is all that is great by
love or hatred, by feeling or thought, by knowledge
or power, by happiness or unhappiness, by the future
or by the past."

Among the "notabilities" spoken of by the
German poet and chronicler Jenny Lind was anxious
to range herself. But she did not yet consider herself fitted to compete with the greatest singers of
the day; and Paris had at that time a well-appointed

Italian Opera, with Grisi and Persiani among the vocalists, as well as the so-called Académie Royale de Musique, or Grand Opera. At Paris, then, her first visit was to the famous professor of singing, Manuel Garcia, for many years past better known in London than in Paris; who, after hearing her, recommended her to take a long period of repose. For several weeks, or even months, the young vocalist left to Nature the task of repairing the ravages caused in her voice by premature exertion. Then she visited Garcia again; and he put her through a course of study, at the end of which he considered her fit to undertake an engagement for principal parts, at the Paris Opera-house. Different accounts have been published as to what now took place. The German musical lexicographer, Mendel, declares that Jenny Lind appeared publicly at the Paris Opera, and sang without success. Larousse, in his "Dictionnaire du Dix-Neuvième Siècle," repeats Mendel's error; and it is to be observed that neither in the German nor in the French dictionary is the name given of the opera in which Jenny Lind is said to have appeared. If from Mendel, less accurate than German editors generally are, and from Larousse, more accurate than French editors are generally supposed to be, we turn to the almost invariably correct Castil Blaze, we find a detailed account of a trial performance said to have been gone through by Jenny Lind at the Paris Opera with a view to an engagement, which, however, was not at the time offered to her. The following, according to the historian of the Académie Royale de Musique, is what really took place:—

In the autumn of 1840, strongly recommended by Garcia and by Meyerbeer, Jenny Lind applied for an engagement at the Paris Opera-house. Mdlle. Falcon, after succeeding Madame Dorus-Gras as " Alice " in *Robert le Diable,* and in other analogous parts, had in her turn left the theatre, and it was natural to suppose that a new and competent representative of the characters which Mdlle. Falcon had now abandoned would be welcomed, or, at least, not unfavourably received.

But the director of the Paris Opera-house, M. Léon Pillet, was just then unduly interested in the artistic success and general welfare of Madame Stolz; and it was not thought desirable to engage a new soprano when the reigning favourite possessed a contralto voice and was on the look out for leading contralto parts. It was for Madame Stolz that about this time the part of " Léonore " in Donizetti's opera of *La Favorite,* was specially composed, so that M. Léon Pillet's " favouritism " (so to say) produced at least one good result. But while increasing the operatic repertory of Europe by one second-class work, it prevented the French public from hearing one of the first singers of her time.

Meyerbeer had arranged that a hearing should be given to Mdlle. Lind in the concert-room of the Opera-house. The orchestra was present, and she sang to full accompaniment three operatic scenes; those of " Agatha " (*Der Freyschütz*), of " Alice " (*Robert le Diable*), and of " Norma." No better scheme could have been devised for exhibiting the talent of the young vocalist in three very different parts. But neither the singing of Jenny Lind nor its approval by Meyerbeer was of any avail. The so-called trial performance was but an empty farce. Madame Stolz would tolerate no rival in the domain over which she ruled; and without this lady's permission M. Léon Pillet was afraid to make a step. Justly susceptible, Jenny Lind did not forgive the slight. The *spretæ injuria vocis* was felt; and when seven or eight years later, after her brilliant success in London, an engagement was offered to her at the Paris Opera-house, she refused it without assigning any definite reason.

So far M. Castil Blaze. He is right in saying that Jenny Lind never made a public appearance at the Grand Opera of Paris ; right also in saying that she went through a trial performance at that theatre in presence of Meyerbeer; and apparently right, moreover, in saying that M. Léon Pillet did not think it likely that Madame Stolz and Jenny Lind would be able to get on together as members of the same company.

According, however, to M. Léon Pillet, who, on retiring from the management of the Académie Royale de Musique, published in 1847 a brief account of his four years' management, there was never any question of Jenny Lind's being engaged at the Paris Opera-house. But let him speak in his own words. This, then, is what M. Léon Pillet says in his pamphlet of eighty-three pages, entitled: "Académie Royale de Musique. Compte rendu de la gestion depuis le 1er juin, 1840, jusqu'an 1er juin, 1846":—

"Much has been said about Mdlle. Lind. It has been asserted —

"I. That Meyerbeer presented her to me himself four years ago, and that I refused to engage her.

"II. That since her success in Germany he had in vain pressed me to engage her. It has even been said that Mdlle. Lind herself applied for an engagement; and in some theatrical journals the very sum she is said to have asked, and which, it is said, I refused, has been given.

"There are so many fables, as to which I may as well set forth the truth.

"Four years ago, *i.e.*, 1843, at the time when Meyerbeer was seeking, not a soprano, but a tenor for *Le Prophète*, he came to me just before leaving Paris and asked me to let him hear on the stage a young person who had been much praised to him.

'It is not for you,' he hastened to answer. 'She is said to have a pretty voice, but not strong enough for the Grand Opera. I want to see if it will be of any use for Berlin.'

"I gave Meyerbeer all the facilities he had asked for; placing at his disposition, not only the stage, but an accompanist (M. Benoit). Then I myself took him on to the stage with Mdlle. Lind, whom I expected to hear, when suddenly I was told that the committee, which still used to meet at the Opera, wished to see me.

"I accordingly apologized to Meyerbeer and Mdlle. Lind, and then left them without hearing a single note. The next day I asked what Meyerbeer had thought of his singer. He said, I was told, that she was not without talent, but that she had still much to learn.

"That did not show that she had produced a great impression upon him; and he, indeed, thought so little of her then for the opera that he did not even mention her to me. It was only last year at Cologne that, talking of Mdlle. Lind, he reminded me of the circumstance which I have just related.

"As for the other assertion that Meyerbeer had afterwards pressed me in vain to engage this singer, it is as incorrect as the first.

"Meyerbeer did, indeed, say to me last winter that he had the highest opinion of this artist's

talent; that if it was possible to have her and
Madame Stolz at the same theatre it would be
admirable. But, he hastened to add, he thought it
impossible; that the same thing would happen
probably as with Nourrit and Duprez; that being
both sufficiently strong to occupy the first place at
a theatre, neither of them would consent to hold a
secondary position; that, moreover, Mdlle. Lind's
pecuniary demands would be very considerable, and
that as far as he was concerned he should be quite
content to have for the second part in the *Prophète*
Mdlle. Brambilla or Madame Rossi-Caccia.

"In order to have a clear conscience, however, I
begged him to ask Mdlle. Lind if she would consent
to leave the land of her triumphs for an engagement
at Paris. He refused to undertake this commission.

"I was about to make the proposition myself,
although without much hope, when M. Vatel (at
that time director of the Italian Theatre), who had
had the same idea as myself, communicated to me
the following letter, which he had just received :—

"'Monsieur le Directeur,

"'I have had the honour to receive your
letter of the 13th November, and I beg you to forgive me for having left you so long without a reply.
But before answering it was necessary for me to
reflect.

"'I have decided, sir, to remain in Germany

during the short time that I shall appear on the stage.

"'For the more I think of it the more I am convinced that I am not for Paris nor Paris for me.

"'I leave the theatre in a year from now, and until then I have so much to do in Germany that I cannot accept any engagement either for Paris or for London.

"'Permit me, however, to express to you my gratitude for having thought me worthy to appear before the first public in the world ; and let me assure you, Monsieur le Directeur, that I do you the least harm in not incurring the risk of a failure.

"'Believe me, etc.,

"'(Signed) JENNY LIND.'"

From Paris Jenny Lind had returned to Stockholm, where, on her reappearance at the Court Theatre, she was received with unbounded enthusiasm. In 1843 she started once more on her travels, and in the spring of that year accepted an engagement at Copenhagen. From Copenhagen she went back once more to her native Stockholm. But Scandinavia was too small. Her ambition embraced the whole of Europe—not to speak of America, to which, as yet, she had probably never given a thought. She wrote to Meyerbeer, whose acquaintance she had made at Paris, and the composer of *Robert le Diable* procured for her an engage-

ment as second soprano at the Royal Opera-house
of Berlin. Here she made her first appearance as
" Adalgisa " in *Norma;* but it was not until she took
the part of " Alice" that she produced any deep
impression on the Berlin public. The purity and
simplicity of this character were indeed perfectly
suited both to her nature and to her artistic style.
So great was the effect produced by Jenny Lind as
the peasant heroine of Meyerbeer's opera that news
of it soon reached London; and in a very few
weeks an emissary arrived at Berlin bearing pro-
posals on the part of Mr. Benjamin Lumley, at that
time manager of Her Majesty's Theatre. No definite
engagement, however, seems to have been offered,
and none, in any case, was accepted. Meanwhile
the Swedish vocalist was gradually acquiring a
European reputation. Meyerbeer entrusted to her
at Dresden the part of " Vielka" in his *Camp of
Silesia,* afterwards with many modifications to become *L'Etoile du Nord;* and here she appeared as
" Amina," " Norma " and " Maria," parts in which
she was soon to be heard at Her Majesty's Theatre.

Vienna was the scene of her next great triumphs,
and in 1846 she once more received propositions
from London. This time it was Mr. Bunn, manager
of Drury Lane Theatre, who wished to secure her
services; and with him she signed a formal contract. Immediately afterwards a new offer arrived

from Mr. Lumley; and preferring, in accordance with the representations of her friends, Her Majesty's Theatre to Drury Lane, she put aside Mr. Bunn and agreed to sing for Mr. Lumley. A sum of two thousand pounds offered to Mr. Bunn by way of compensation was refused; and for some time the action for damages with which the popular vocalist was threatened by the disappointed manager afforded abundant material to the gossips of London. It may here be mentioned that in due time Mr. Bunn's action was brought, the Court awarding him by way of damages five hundred pounds more than the sum that had been tendered to him.

Jenny Lind sang for the first time in London May 4th, 1847. The opera was *Robert le Diable,* and the cast comprised Fraschini as " Robert ; " Gardoni as " Raimbaud " (the part in which Mario at the Paris Opera-house made his first appearance on the stage) ; Staudigl as " Bertram ; " Castellan as " Isabelle ; " and Jenny Lind as " Alice." The house was densely crowded; though, according to the *Musical World,* the speculators in seats had so overdone the business that several boxes were left without occupants. " Jenny Lind," says a writer in the journal just cited, " is young, of the middle height, fair-haired, blue-eyed, neither stout nor slender, but well proportioned, neither fat nor thin, but enough of the one for comeliness, and enough of the other for romance, meek looking when her features are at rest, full of animation and energy when they are at play—like Fate when she frowns, like love when she smiles—in short the very maiden of the German poet's dreams, the Jungfrau of Schiller's ideal. Jenny Lind is neither handsome nor plain, neither pretty nor ugly, but something that hovers about the abstract qualities of everything, catching a portion of them, but resembling them in nothing." In this not very direct, nor altogether intelligible description of Jenny Lind's vague attractiveness is nevertheless indicated the character of her peculiar charm.

The second part undertaken by Jenny Lind at Her Majesty's Theatre was that of " Amina" in *La Sonnambula;* and before the season closed the new prima donna had also been heard as " Maria " in *La Fille du Régiment*, as "Norma," and as "Susanna" in *Le Nozze di Figaro*. In 1848 she returned and added to her Anglo-Italian repertory " Lucia " in Donizetti's opera, " Adina " in *L'Elisir*, and " Elvira " in *I Puritani*. In the winter of 1848, Jenny Lind undertook a tour in the provinces; and, according to Mr. Lumley, her share in the profits amounted to £10,000. But in the course of the winter it was rumoured that the "Swedish Nightingale" had resolved to leave the stage. Mr. Lumley could secure no contract from her except to give a series of six opera recitals at Her Majesty's, "without scenery, dresses, or decorations."

The first recital, of Mozart's *Magic Flute*, took place April 15th, 1849; and it was also the last. The house was comparatively empty, and the audience, which during the "Jenny Lind fever" had been enthusiastic enough, was quite cold. A failure such as this overcame the scruples of the artist, and the prima donna exercised the lady's privilege of changing her mind. On April 26th she reappeared in *Sonnambula*. One performance each of "Lucia" and "La Figlia" followed; and on May 18th, 1849, as "Alice" in *Roberto*, the fascinating prima donna made her last appearance on any stage.

Mr. Lumley, with a formidable opposition to encounter from the recently founded Royal Italian Opera, was determined to give his new prima donna every chance. He asked Verdi to compose an opera specially for her; and the result was *I Masnadieri*, produced under the composer's personal direction, with Jenny Lind in the principal part. This work, it may be added, founded on Schiller's *Robbers*, is now entirely and deservedly forgotten. The characters in which Jenny Lind appeared at Her Majesty's Theatre have been already mentioned. It has already, moreover, been set forth that her operatic career in England lasted but two seasons, and that with her second London season her career as

an operatic singer came to an end.   Her performances in America must, of course, not be forgotten,
though they added less, perhaps, to her reputation
than to that of Mr. Barnum ; who, abandoning for a
time his waxworks, wild beasts, and various kinds
of human monstrosities, became for a brief season,
in view of the money to be made out of the Swedish
nightingale, a veritable impresario.

Mr. Barnum is generally credited with an un-
usual degree of smartness.   But Mr. Frith, in his
recently published memoirs, tells a story of him
which proves that, smart or not, he was fair and
even generous.   On arriving in America Jenny
Lind found that the terms she had made with Mr.
Barnum were not so advantageous as they might
have been ; but she was bound by her contract, and
in default of a release was prepared to fulfil its conditions. " Immediately after the lady's arrival,"
writes Mr. Frith, " Mr. Barnum appeared.   He
listened to reasons and explanations, all demon-
strating from the singer's point of view the
mistake that had been made ; and he was assured
that if those reasons had no weight with him he
might rely upon every point of the engagement
being religiously carried out.

" ' This, madam, is the document you signed in
England, is it not ? ' said Mr. Barnum, producing a
deed.

" ' Undoubtedly,' said the lady, ' and I am ready
to abide by it if I have been unable to convince—'

" ' Be so good as to destroy it. Tear it up,
madam; and if you will instruct your lawyer to
prepare another from your own dictation, naming
whatever you think fair for your services, I will
sign it without hesitation.'

" ' I remember my first meeting with the famous
songstress,' said Mr. Barnum, after Jenny Lind's
death. ' . . . It was on Sunday morning, Sept. 1st,
1850, on board the steamer *Atlantic* at quarantine,
where I slept all night in the residence of Dr. A. S.
Boane, then the health officer. After a few moments'
conversation with her she asked me where I had
heard her sing. " I never had the pleasure of seeing you before in my life," I replied. " How is it
possible that you dared risk so much money on a
person whom you never heard sing ? " she asked, in
surprise. " I risked it on your reputation, which, in
musical matters, I would much rather have than my
own judgment," I answered. Although I relied
upon Jenny Lind's reputation as a great musical
artist, I also took largely into my estimate of her
success with all classes of the American public her
character for extraordinary benevolence and generosity. Without this peculiarity in her disposition I

never would have dared make the engagement which I did.'

" . . . Jenny Lind's character for benevolence became so generally known that her door was beset by persons asking charity; and she was in the receipt, while in the principal cities, of numerous letters, all on the same subject. I know of many instances in which she gave sums of money to applicants varying from £4, £10, and £100 to £200, and once she gave £1,000 to a Swedish friend.

" Jenny was in the habit of attending church whenever she could do so without attracting notice. She always preserved her nationality, and always attended Swedish churches whenever they could be found. She gave £200 to a Swedish church in Chicago. While in Baltimore, my daughter Caroline, who was mistaken for Jenny, went to church and sang in the choir. ' What an exquisite singer!' ' Heavenly sounds!' ' I never heard the like!' and similar expressions were whispered through the church. A funny incident, involving Horace Greely, occurred upon Jenny's arrival in New York. She was received at the Irving House that stood on the north-west corner of Broadway and Chambers Street. Greely came over with his trousers tucked into his boots and wearing his proverbial light-coloured overcoat. He started to remove his over-

coat when a friend said, ' Don't ! it will destroy
your identity.' * So he wore it to the room where
Jenny was, and after an introduction she said, ' I
have heard so much about that overcoat that I
would not have known you without it.' Jenny
Lind gave ninety-five concerts while in America,
and the aggregate receipts were £142,432, averag-
ing about £1,500. The net receipts amounted to
£35,000 odd. Of her half of the receipts of the
first two concerts she devoted £2,000 to charity in
New York. She afterwards gave charity concerts
in various cities."

On landing at New York Jenny Lind found
herself at once surrounded by crowds of enthusiastic admirers, who had never, indeed, heard her
sing, but who had read rapturous accounts of the
effect her singing produced on others. She was
hailed as a great European celebrity, and the day of
her arrival it would be no small distinction even to
have seen her. She drove to her hotel, and would
probably have retired to rest, for it was already
nearly midnight ; but at twelve o'clock some
30,000 persons assembled in front of the Irving
House, where she had put up, and at the agreeable
hour of one in the morning a band of one hundred

---

* I once met Mr. Horace Greely in Paris, when his identity
was marked by a singularly bad hat, which he told me he had worn
across the Atlantic and in all weathers.

and thirty musicians, preceded by 700 members of the Fire Brigade, came to serenade her.

In view of the great demand for tickets it was decided to sell them to the highest bidder, and those who wished to hear Jenny Lind at her first concert had to compete at auction for the honour. The newspapers thought it interesting to publish a *facsimile* of the concert tickets, and they printed the names of those who had secured the best places.

The extravagant purchaser of the first ticket sold by auction for the first of Jenny Lind's concerts in America was a hatter named Genin, who, entering into the spirit of Mr. Barnum's ingenious device, turned it to account for his own particular benefit. It was, of course, for advertising purposes, and in order that his name might be proclaimed throughout the length and breadth of the American Continent, that Mr. Genin gave two hundred and twenty-five dollars for his stall ; and for some days his name was as well known as that of the great singer herself. It was an insane thing, all the same, to give so much money for a concert ticket ; and it is possibly from Mr. Genin's famous investment that the proverb " Mad as a hatter " is derived.

Those who could not afford the luxury of hearing Jenny Lind were anxious, at least, to see her ; and whenever she drove out she was followed by crowds, which sometimes degenerated into mobs. Public receptions, too, were arranged for her, at which she presided like a queen, though with less formality.

The famous singer made her first appearance before an American audience at Castle Garden, 11th September, 1850. The concert hall was crowded in every part, and when the " Swedish nightingale" stepped on to the platform she was saluted by an audience of 7,000 persons, who shouted most vociferously. Her principal solo was " Casta Diva," from *Norma*. She sang with Belletti, the baritone, in the duet from Rossini's *Turco in Italia;* and she was also heard in the trio for soprano voice and two flutes from Meyerbeer's *Camp of Silesia,* afterwards transplanted to *L'Etoile du Nord*, where it now figures. The programme moreover contained some Swedish national airs, in which the singer created as much enthusiasm as in any of her operatic pieces.

Out of the 26,000 dollars realized by this concert, Jenny Lind gave her share of the profits—10,000 dollars—to the principal New York charities ; and this was but the first of many like donations made by her during her tour in the United States.

At Boston the celebrated vocalist sang for the first time on the 1st of October, and here, at the Tremont Temple, she renewed the success which she had gained at New York. Her professional visits included Philadelphia, Baltimore, Washington, Richmond, Charleston, and Havana. The tour was but a limited one, compared with those made thirty-five years later by Madame Adelina Patti. But in Jenny Lind's days there was no railway through the Rocky Mountains; nor was California worth visiting at a time when San Francisco scarcely existed.

At Baltimore the adored vocalist was bowing one evening from the balcony of her hotel to a crowd which had assembled to applaud her. She somehow dropped her shawl; when, instead of restoring it, her admirers tore it to shreds and chivalrously pocketed the pieces.

In June, 1851, after paying a stipulated forfeit of 30,000 dollars, Jenny Lind separated herself from Mr. Barnum, her ingenious and enterprising business partner, and soon afterwards chose as her partner for life Mr. Otto Goldschmidt, a pianist of considerable ability, who, during the latter part of her tour, had accompanied her in a double sense. Mr. Otto Goldschmidt had played with success in London at the concerts of the Musical Union, and after his return to England he produced an oratorio on the subject of " Ruth."

Madame Goldschmidt left America in 1852. During her various American tours she had gained enormous sums of money, of which a good portion was distributed by her in donations and endowments. After making ample provision for her parents, she had still a very large capital at her own disposal. Since her first appearance at Her Majesty's Theatre she had sung for only two seasons on the stage, and she seemed now to have decided to relinquish even concert singing. On no terms could she be prevailed upon to sing when, on her return from America, she passed through England on her way to Germany. Here she settled for a time at Dresden, where, it will be remembered, she had sung eight years before in Meyerbeer's *Camp of Silesia.*

In 1856, however, she came back to London, and accepted an engagement for oratorio at Exeter Hall. But a singer who abandons opera for operatic concerts, and operatic concerts for oratorio, is on the way towards not singing at all; and after her appearances at Exeter Hall, beginning late in 1856 and ending early in 1857, Jenny Lind retired into private life, from which she was never again to emerge, except at rare intervals, to sing on some special occasion for charitable purposes.

The American tour played an important part in Jenny Lind's life; for we have seen that in the United States she made the acquaintance of Mr. Otto Goldschmidt, her future husband. Much was said during the tour in America about her charitable gifts, but far less than the facts would have justified. Her profits from the tour were immense, and so also were the sums which she spent in founding musical scholarships and in contributing to the support of benevolent institutions. After her return to Europe in 1852 Madame Lind-Goldschmidt gave concerts, but sang no more on the stage. Some years later she interested herself in the Bach choir, whose performances were directed by her husband; and when the Royal College of Music was started she volunteered her services as a teacher of singing. That they were readily accepted need scarcely be added. In private life Madame Lind-Goldschmidt was much esteemed; and by those who knew her personally she will be remembered as an ornament, not only of the concert-room and above all of the operatic stage, but of the society, everywhere, in which she moved.

Although such musicians as Mendelssohn, Meyer-beer, and Moscheles were enthusiastic in their admiration of Jenny Lind, critics, and critics of eminence, were found who, oddly enough, or, as some will say, naturally enough, professed themselves not altogether satisfied with her.

" There surely," said an esteemed writer in the *Musical World*, " never was such a fuss about any one individual in the world of árt." Elsewhere the same writer observes : " The Catalani fever was nothing to it, the Sontag fever nothing to it, even the Paganini fever was a fool to it. So great is the turmoil, so terrible the confusion, so furious the whirlwind, so plentiful the dust, that not a critic but is blind as the public, and gropes about in the dark chamber of sophism, dealing buffets right and left, sometimes hitting upon the wall of truth, but as often stumbling against the chairs and tables of chicanery. We own that, like our brothers of the goose-quill, we have been strangely bothered. Something has given our judgment a sprain, and it is for the nonce incapable of exercising its functions. And so we have fallen in with the crowd; but for the life of us we cannot undertake to swear whether we be in the right or whether we be in the wrong."

Mr. Chorley made a point of showing that he could not allow himself to be carried away by the general enthusiasm, and he wrote on the subject ("Musical Recollections of the Last Half-Century") : "To my ear she invariably sang somewhat sharp, and I could by no means consider any prima donna to be a great artist who was only positively successful in four operas—*Roberto, La Sonnambula, La Figlia del Reggimento,* and *Le Nozze di Figaro,* her 'Norma' having been a complete failure."

It may be more interesting to see what opinion was entertained of Jenny Lind by the great musicians with whom she came in contact. Beginning with her childhood Sir Julius Benedict wrote of her in *Scribner's Magazine* (May, 1881) :—

"Without personal attractions, deprived even of the simplest enjoyments of childhood, she sought and found in music a little world of her own in which she could forget the entire absence of true motherly affection and the many other troubles of her dismal home.

"She succeeded in making her naturally harsh and unbending organ supple and pliant. To acquire by dint of unceasing study the most perfect shake; to blend the different registers of her voice so skilfully as effectually to conceal any break; to execute passages and runs with a full, rich tone, instead of the thin, wiry quality which generally belongs to bravura singers; to be infallible in her intonation —these were the great aims she accomplished."

The trio for voice and two flutes in the *Camp of Silesia*, chiefly associated later on with Adelina Patti in *L'Etoile du Nord*, gave rise to "frantic demonstrations." Moscheles was present on one occasion, and thus referred to it in a private letter: "Jenny Lind has fairly enchanted me. She is unique in her way, and her song with two concertante flutes is perhaps the most incredible feat in the way of bravura singing that can possibly be heard." Moscheles, indeed, showed himself no less fascinated by Jenny Lind than Meyerbeer

before him. When on a visit to London in 1847
he thus wrote to his friends in Germany : " What
shall I say of Jenny Lind ? I can find no words
adequate to give you any real idea of the impression
she has made. Independently of the fact that the
language of panegyric is exhausted, this wonderful
artist stands too high in my judgment to be dragged
down by common-place complimentary phrases, such
as newspaper writers so copiously indulge in. . . .
I wanted to know her off the stage as well as on,
but as she lives some distance from me I asked her in
a letter to fix upon an hour for me to call. Simple
and unceremonious as she is, she came the next day
herself, bringing her answer verbally. So much
modesty and so much greatness united are seldom
to be met with ; and, although her intimate friend,
Mendelssohn, had given me an insight into her noble
character, I was surprised to find them so apparent
on first acquaintance. I had to play her my fantasia
on her Swedish songs. Mendelssohn had chosen the
subjects with me, and she said many pretty things
about my characteristic treatment of her national
airs. We returned her visit at Old Brompton, where
she lives far from the noise of the capital and the
arena of her brilliant performances."

When it was proposed by the Birmingham Festival Committee that Mendelssohn should offer
her an engagement for the forthcoming *Elijah,*

he replied: "If you can have Jenny Lind for the festival, by all means have her, for there is now no singer on the continent to be compared to her. But although she has no fixed engagement neither at Berlin or elsewhere, I fear it will be difficult to make her come, as they are all mad about her and force her into more engagements than she can accept."

When the Committee urged that Mendelssohn himself should write to her, he answered: "Your question about Jenny Lind is very important to the success of the Festival, as I consider her, without hesitation, the first singer of the day, and perhaps of many days to come. But I am not able to undertake the negotiation which your chairman would entrust me with, as I know how much she is surrounded with engagements of all sorts, and how little likely it is that I could get a positive answer from her, unless a formal application from the Committee had previously been made to her. It is by no means certain that such an application would be successful, but, at any rate, I think it the only way if there is one. When you formerly wrote to me about the same subject I was at Berlin, and spoke to her about it, but then she said she should not go to England; she had declined already twice, so I am sure she will not come to London at least. . . . At present I am afraid by beginning to

talk or correspond with Jenny Lind about this subject I should do your cause no good, and I therefore
beg to be excused."

I have quoted Sir Julius Benedict's opinion about
this marvellous singer, and to his article in
Scribner I must again turn for an account of the
reasons which made her retire from the stage.

Sir Julius states that " the principal cause of her
retirement was the objection of a gentleman to whom
she was engaged—an engagement afterwards broken
off—to her further appearance on the stage." He
mentions also another reason likely to have exercised
a very powerful influence. " It cannot be denied,"
he says, " that it was only in five parts she held an
undisputed sway over her audiences. . . . Her sphere
being thus limited, it was natural that she should
hesitate before continuing her theatrical engagements, feeling, as she did, the immense responsibility
of maintaining a position so exceptional, so glorious,
but also so dangerous. . . . Her strength did not
equal her ambition, which was almost as great as
her talent. When on the stage, and in order that
nothing should interfere with what she looked upon
as her mission, she would give up all the pleasures of
social intercourse, invariably refusing dinners and
evening parties, and sacrificing the best years of her
life to her feeling of duty. How often did she tell
me that, knowing what the public had a right to

expect from her, and being fully aware that any
shortcomings in her performances would destroy the
prestige she had acquired after so many years of
trial, she felt that she could not continue the strain
for any length of time without being crushed beneath
the weight of the self-created difficulties of her
position.   The exacting demands of opera and concert goers had been so exceptionally raised, not only
by her own merit, but by often injudicious eulogies
in the Press, that each of her new characters was
looked forward to as a necessary improvement on all
its predecessors.   Unless the already over-anxious
artist had thrown all her soul into the impersonation
of new works, there would have been an outcry of a
diminution in her efficiency.   Such constant excitement was too much for her physical and moral
strength, and thus her resolution to abandon the
scene of her triumphs became almost a necessity."

The chroniclers of the period say but little upon the
subject of Jenny Lind's impersonation of " Lucia."
According to Sir Julius Benedict, however, it was
one of her best parts.   " Who," he asks, " having
seen Jenny Lind in ' Lucia,' can ever forget the expression of mental agony, the fixed look of threaten-
ing insanity, the stifled voice of a heart rent in twain
by despair, and rising to an almost painful climax of
hopeless passion, in her last scene, when, in her
madness, she is recalling the vows of her lover and

her own dream of happiness ? . . . Where she stood,
however, alone and unrivalled, and where the most
difficult judge could hardly detect a flaw, was in the
part of ' Alice ' and of the ' Figlia.' The whole
conception of the simple French peasant girl was a
histrionic and musical achievement such as has rarely
been seen or heard. In another style similar praise
must be awarded to the representation of the adopted
daughter of the regiment. Every *nuance*, from
mutinous archness to the most emphatic expression
of grief, a variety of vocal effects—now a dazzling
display of bravura, now an unassuming melody—
left no room for criticism."

Having cited some slightly supercilious criticisms
of Jenny Lind's singing from the pen of Mr. Chorley,
I may, by way of counterpoise, and, as an act of
justice to the writer, appeal from Chorley affected
and hypercritical, to Chorley natural and appreciative.

" Of all the singers whom I have ever heard," he
once wrote, " Mdlle. Lind was, perhaps, the most
assiduous. Her resolution to offer the very best of
her best to her public seemed part and parcel of her
nature, and of her conscience. Not a note was
neglected by her—not a phrase slurred over. . . .
Her execution was great, and, as is always the case
with voices originally reluctant, seemed greater than
it really was. Her shake was true and brilliant;

her taste in ornament was altogether original. . . .
She used her pianissimo tones so as to make them
resemble an effect of ventriloquism. . . . The wild,
queer northern tunes brought here by her, her care-
ful expression of some of Mozart's great airs, her
mastery over such a piece as ' The Bird Song ' in
Haydn's *Creation,* and, lastly, the grandeur of inspiration with which the ' Sanctus ' in Mendelssohn's
Elijah was led by her, are so many things to leave
on the mind of all who have heard them, so many
indelible prints. These are the triumphs, in my
poor judgment, which will stamp Madame Lind-
Goldschmidt's name in the Golden Book of Singers."

One of the most valuable and most interesting
books on the subject of music and musicians, Moscheles' " Life," contains many passages concerning
Jenny Lind, her charming disposition and her delightful singing.

" Mendelssohn," he says in one place, " took
good care not to miss the children's party at
Moscheles' house. Our conversation was purely
on musical subjects, whilst the others laughed and
played with the children. I had to put before him
an offer from Chappell, who wanted to have the
copyright of an opera which he was to write. The
subject proposed was *The Tempest;* the opera was
to be in the regular Italian style, for Lumley. Not
a note has been written, and yet the work is already

announced for Jenny Lind's appearance in the coming season. Later on Mendelssohn completely abandoned the plan of setting music to the subject, and wrote to say so, to the disappointment of the Directors."

In lieu of the opera on the subject of *The Tempest* which Mendelssohn was to have composed, a not very brilliant work on the same theme by Halévy was brought out.

After Jenny Lind's marriage to Mr. Otto Gold-schmidt, Moscheles heard her sing at Leipsic, and thus describes the event —

"One thing that was joyfully welcomed by all of us at Leipzig was the appearance here of the Lind-Goldschmidts, for the first time since their marriage. Madame Lind-Goldschmidt sang for the ' Pension Fund,' and was our star at the subscription concert. She can tone down her glorious voice to a pianissimo whisper, and the sound, however attenuated, is distinctly audible in the remotest corner of the Concert Room. She is wonderfully versatile. After astounding everyone with her ' fiori-ture,' and stirring all hearts with her deeply expres-sive singing, she becomes at once exquisitely naïve, and sings a ' Kinderlied ' by Taubert, or the ' Son-nenschein ' in a style that makes her hearers feel young again. Goldschmidt played in a great deal of beautiful music. In Chopin's Concertos, Mendelssohn's 'Variations Sérieuses,' a prelude by Bach, and some drawing-room pieces, he proved himself a genuine artist, earnest and thorough, with no straining for show or effect. I was so glad to be able to be of service to him, and to prove my great respect and esteem for him, by lending him my Erard piano."

Again Moscheles writes : " We have passed some delightful hours with the Goldschmidts, meeting them at a friendly dinner and at a *matinée* given by Preusser, where Otto Goldschmidt played his trio, a well-written, clear, and melodious composition, which gave me great pleasure. The Goldschmidts paid us a visit at the Conservatoire, and seemed perfectly satisfied with the performances of the pupils, especially that of the youthful Fritz Gernsheim, who highly distinguished himself in Mendelssohn's 'Serenade' and 'Allegro.' Madame Goldschmidt repeatedly expressed her esteem for an institution to which her husband owed his musical education, and this she did not only in words but in songs as well, for she sang Mendelssohn's Psalm, 'Hear my prayer,' so exquisitely that none who heard it can ever forget the impression she created."

Jenny Lind has been made the heroine of a good many anecdotes, nor has their number decreased since her death. It is said that on one occasion, when she sang for the first time at Vienna, the audience insisted, as usual, on hearing her sing a second time the popular *rondo finale* of *La Sonnambula*. She was very tired, but at the same time very anxious to oblige the public. She accordingly walked up to the footlights and exclaimed, with an imploring look: " Five minutes for lemonade ! " What could be done but grant the delay so pathetically demanded? The five minutes soon passed away, and Jenny Lind, refreshed and enlivened, attacked " Non Giunge" with the most brilliant effect.

When Jenny Lind first came to England Mr. Lumley had made it one of the conditions of her engagement that she should sing nowhere except at his theatre, and to this rule there were to be no exceptions. Accordingly, when Her Majesty requested her (commanded would, I believe, be the more accurate word) to sing at the Palace she could only reply by an apology. Jenny Lind was afraid, however, lest the Queen should think her ungrateful. She accordingly drove to Buckingham Palace, gave her card to one of the sentries, and desired that it might be carried to Queen Victoria. The proper functionary was sent for, and he was just explaining how impossible it was for him to announce Mdlle. Lind, when someone of superior authority interfered and took the card to the Queen. Notwithstanding the informality of her visit, Jenny Lind was at once received.

Jenny Lind, a typical daughter of the North, had nothing Southern or Oriental in her nature. She cannot, then, like the Grisis, the Pastas, the Garcias, and (to such a point can ethnical arrogance be carried) like Rossini, be claimed as of Jewish race; but it was her destiny throughout her public career to be surrounded, influenced, and greatly benefited by Jews. She created the part of "Ruth" in her husband's oratorio, and the Jews may well regard her as one who, like the Moabite maiden, was a stranger in the midst of the chosen people.

Among musicians of eminence, Meyerbeer was the first to appreciate and befriend her. He arranged for her, at the Paris Opera-house, that trial performance which, through no fault on his part, did not lead to a public appearance; and it was Meyerbeer who got her engaged at the Berlin Opera-house, and who, at Dresden, in his *Camp of Silesia*, gave her for the first time an opportunity of creating an original part. Moscheles, another Jew, who was afterwards to become one of her warmest friends, heard her in the *Camp of Silesia*, and immediately afterwards wrote to his wife: "Jenny Lind has truly enchanted me; " while Mendelssohn, who was one of the most enthusiastic of all her admirers, said of her in one of his letters : " In my whole life I have not seen an artistic nature so noble, so genuine, so true as is that of Jenny Lind. Natural gifts, study, and depth of feeling I have never seen united in the same degree ; and, although one of these qualities may have been more prominent in other persons, the combination of all three has never existed before."

Jenny Lind's London manager was Mr. Benjamin Lumley, a Jew ; and when she started for America she was accompanied, as musical conductor of the tour, by Benedict, also a Jew. The sixth of the Jews whom she was to number among her friends and to place above all the others was Mr. Otto Goldschmidt, whom she met during the American tour and married before it came to an end.

Jenny Lind, one of the sweetest singers and most charming women of our time, died peacefully Nov. 2nd, 1887, at Malvern Wells, where she had built herself a house and made herself a home. " My last remembrance," writes Canon Holland in the interesting and touching account of Jenny Lind contributed by him to *Murray's Magazine* (Dec., 1887), " is of her kindly waving her hand in good-bye as she sat in her great chair, very white but still impressive and vigorous, with the sweet English hills and woods about her steeped in delicious sunlight.

"Shortly after she became worse, and never left her bed again. She was almost too weak to speak, but her daughter, who hardly ever left her during all this pitiful time, wrote to me that one morning as they drew the blinds to let her beloved sun stream in upon her, she sang three or four bars of Schumann's *Sonnenschein.* She longed to die, and hoped eagerly that it might be on her birthday, October 6th, but her great vitality dragged on the long struggle, and not until November 2nd, All Hallows' Day, did her soul pass away with a few soft sighs. She was buried amid the sweetest music, sung by the choirs in Malvern Abbey Church, and with wreaths and flowers which not only loaded the hearse, but filled a separate car. So they laid her body to rest under the Malvern Hills, and 'over her grave' (says one) 'it seemed as if the very birds would sing more sweetly than elsewhere.' For the music in her was ever an inspiration, which lifted her as the lark is carried heavenward by its song—the lark, her own chosen symbol, carved over her house-door; the lark, the winged thing that 'singing ever soars,' and 'soaring ever sings.'"

CHAPTER II.

BOSIO.

OTHER singers as accomplished, as graceful, as fascinating as Bosio may since her death have appeared; but with her died a number of characters which, to the more ancient of opera-goers, will always be associated with her memory.

There is no such " merciless invoker of the ghosts of the past " as music; and there are certain melodies which will always recall more forcibly than any painting could do the girlish figure, the artless manner, and the exquisite voice of the well-named " Angiolina " Bosio. The happy, spontaneous strain which accompanies the entry of the jester's daughter in *Rigoletto* suggests but one " Gilda; " and no one can ever please again in the *Elixir of Love*, those whose one ideal " Norina" is no more. The true " Zerlina," too, is dead—Auber's no less than Mozart's; and the opera of the *Traviata* again becomes unintelligible now that we have lost the only woman who knew how to invest the part of " Violetta" with a grace and delicacy which, instead of improbable, made the passionate love of " Alfred" appear the most natural in the world.

A mere enumeration of the qualities which distinguished Madame Bosio would not give those who are unfortunate enough never to have heard or seen her any fair idea of her grace or her beauty. Literality kills as surely as the photograph, and one can give no better illustration of the impossibility of " describing" Madame Bosio than by mentioning the fact that all the photographic portraits of her are more unlike the original than such things usually are. A dog or a prize-fighter may be photographed to perfection. But portrait painting by machinery becomes more and more incorrect in proportion to the delicacy and refinement of the model ; and the photographs of Madame Bosio are the most inaccurate ever seen. Raphael's " St. Cecilia" is like her, at least in expression ; because St. Cecilia is the true type of the class to which Angiolina Bosio belonged, and because there must necessarily be a family likeness between all women who are endowed with the most exquisite musical sensibility. Even for one who for several years never at any time or at any place missed an opportunity of hearing Madame Bosio it is difficult to tell what was the colour of her eyes, or the number of her years, at the time of her early death, or the compass of her voice. She always looked young and charming ; and whenever she sang she seemed never to have sung so well before. She poetized every part she undertook. No one ever saw her assume a theatrical pose, or play to the audience, or make any kind of "point." But no one possessing the slightest appreciative power who had seen her as " Gilda " could for many years after her death have cared to hear *Rigoletto* again.

To show what wonderful natural gifts Madame Bosio possessed I may mention a fact which will appear incredible, but which is nevertheless true. The most accomplished 'vocalist in Europe, who never sang more easily than when she was singing the most difficult passages, not only knew nothing of music as a science, but could not even read from notes.

I have mentioned the parts which Madame Bosio made specially her own. If asked to state generally what class of characters she represented with the greatest success, I should reply all that are essentially feminine ; in which category one places neither " Norma," nor " Semiramide," nor " Lucrezia Borgia." She played " Lucrezia " in Paris, and " Semiramide " in St. Petersburg; but she had too gentle and tender a nature to look like either of those personages. Fancy the aforesaid

St. Cecilia in the character of " Lady Macbeth,"
or a dove in the plumage of a hawk. The genius
of Bosio was like that of an elegiac poet; she could
be graceful, tender, touching, but not tragic.

In St. Petersburg, where Madame Bosio received
more applause from the public and more distinguished attention from the Court than any vocalist
who had ever visited the Russian capital before, the
news of her death produced the saddest effect.

In less than two years the St. Petersburg Company had lost its two most distinguished members,
who, in their respective lines, were the greatest
artists in the world.   On the occasion of Alexander
the Second's coronation at Moscow the incomparable
duet in the second act of the *Elixir* was sung by
Madame Bosio and Lablache (Una accompanied by
the Lion), and to such perfection that notwithstanding the rule which forbids applause in the presence
of the Emperor, the audience were quite unable to
restrain their enthusiasm. The names of these
singers belong now to the history of Italian Opera;
and Angiolina Bosio takes rank in the annals of the
past with the tender, sensitive Malibran, who, like
her, was cut off in the prime of her life and in the
fulness of her genius.

The first time I had the happiness of hearing
Madame Bosio was at Moscow in the autumn of
1856, during the festivities in honour of the corona-

tion of the Emperor Alexander II. She was the first prima donna who made any marked impression upon me; and I cannot but associate her with the occasion of my first becoming acquainted with her expressive beauty, her graceful talent.

As interesting, in a different way, though less fascinating than the singing of Angiolina Bosio, was the performance, during the co ronation festivities, of the national Russian opera, by Glinka, called *Zisn Za Tsarya,* or, *Life for the Tsar.* Emperors succeed one another on the Russian throne; but Glinka's opera still maintains its prestige, and when Alexander III. ascended the throne *Zisn Za Tsarya* was again laid under contribution, a highly dramatic scene being transferred from the stage to real life, and from the opera, to which it had belonged for nearly fifty years, to the public square on which it actually took place upwards of two centuries and a half ago. The last scene, or epilogue, of Glinka's *Life for the Tsar* represents the triumphal entry into Moscow of the Tsar Michael Fedorovitch, first of the Romanoffs, after the defeat of the Poles, who, having occupied the Russian capital, were driven from it by a general rising of the inhabitants.* But this theatrical

* It is the province of the modern historian to destroy as much as possible the picturesque, the dramatic, the anecdotic character of history; and Professor Kostomaroff has proved that the Polish invaders of 1612 never entered the district inhabited by the hero of Glinka's opera. So much the worse for the facts; the opera still remains.

picture was reproduced, less as a show than as a reality, when Alexander III. entered the Red Square, beneath the battlements of the Kremlin, even as in 1612 it was entered under auspicious circumstances by his ancestor, the founder of the reigning dynasty. Except that the uniform of the troops forming the Imperial escort was entirely different, the scene was in its external features not so much a reproduction as a repetition of the scene of 1612. The peasantry and workmen of Russia wear the same costumes now that they wore in the seventeenth century, and any number of centuries before. The half-picturesque, half-grotesque church of Basil the Blessed stands where it has stood since the days of Ivan the Terrible, a contemporary of Queen Elizabeth ; and the denteated walls of the Kremlin are, in spite of the injuries they received during the fires and explosions of 1812, just what they were when first built as a protection against the Tartars.

The music to which the entry was made, the hymn sung in honour of the newly-crowned Tsar, was new, or at least little more than forty years old. But Glinka has given to his hymn, which is at the same time a march, a thoroughly Russian, and, moreover, a somewhat archaic, character ; and but for the rich harmony and the elaborate, constantly varied instrumentation with which he has beautified and decorated the theme, as he presents it again and again, the theme itself—very simple, very quaint, and, as before said, quite Russian —might certainly belong to the early part of the seventeenth century. Those who have heard Glinka's orchestral scherzo on a national Russian dance-tune called "Kamarinskaia" will remember that the first phrase of that cunningly worked piece consists of only five notes. So also does the first phrase of the Hymn of Triumph in *Life for the Tsar;* and in the second phrase there are peculiarities which, apart from mere simplicity, are decidedly Russian in character. A far better authority on this subject than myself, the late Prince George Galitzin, pointed out some twenty years ago, in his notes to the pro- gramme of a concert of Russian music given by him at St. James's Hall, that Glinka's Hymn of Triumph contains Slavonian elements, whereas the official National Anthem is cosmopolitan in character, suggesting now the Sicilian Mariners' hymn, now that "God Save the Queen" which it served to replace.

According to Prince Galitzin—and the story, true or false, was not invented by him, but has somehow become legendary—the Emperor Nicholas determined one day that Russia must no longer employ on State occasions the "God Save the Queen" of the English, which is also the "Heil dir im Sieger Kranz" of the Prussians, but that she must have a National Anthem

of her own.   The Sovereign who, in reply to an
address from the Holy Synod pointing out that the
Russians prayed for the dead but did not believe in
Purgatory, and asking whether, according to the
doctrine of the Russian Church, Purgatory did or
did not exist, wrote on the margin of the document
at a moment's notice "No Purgatory;" this Sovereign
could not be expected to hesitate very long as to the
choice of a National Anthem.   He called upon
Russian composers to furnish specimens of national
and patriotic music; and from the various hymns,
marches, and anthems sent in, selected two compositions, one by Glinka, the other by Lvoff, for performance in presence of a chosen assembly of courtiers
and dilettanti.   Glinka's hymn and march produced
a good effect, though the fact of its being characteristically Russian was not calculated to help it in
those days, when to be Russian was, with most persons, and especially those of the Court, equivalent to
being vulgar. Lvoff, however, in the orchestral accompaniments to his " God Save the Emperor," had
introduced such a number of trumpets and drums
that Nicholas, touched in his military instincts by
this excessive sonority, was quite carried away, and
in a moment of enthusiasm awarded the victory to
"General" Lvoff, who, it must be explained, owed his
title not to his love of warlike instruments, but to the
grade held by him in the State service.   His office

involved the direction of the choir of the Imperial Chapel and the superintendence of the Court music generally. This had enabled him, in a very literal sense, to gain the ear of the Emperor; and it may have been partly to his own personal influence, and not entirely to the amount of brass and percussion employed in the orchestration of his hymn, that the choice of that hymn was due. It was enough that Glinka's hymn should not have pleased the Emperor above all other hymns for the Slavophils and the malcontents generally in Russia to attach the highest importance to it; which, however, as before pointed out, they were justified in doing on Slavonian and national grounds. Glinka's "Hymn of Triumph," with its thoroughly popular character (for, stripped of its artistic surroundings, it is little more than a Russian dance), came in any case to be looked upon as the National Anthem of Russia in opposition to the State Anthem composed for the Emperor Nicholas with deafening accompaniments of drums and trumpets by the State official, "General" Lvoff. Glinka himself, it may here be explained, was no political malcontent, though, in common with all educated men not in the Government service, he may have been so regarded by the Emperor Nicholas. He was the son of a rich landed proprietor in the neighbourhood of Smolensk, and it was at the house of one of

his relations in the Smolensk province or " government" that he made his first important studies in
music, and above all in orchestration.   This worthy
gentleman, like the Rasoumouskys and the Galitzins,
whose names have been handed down to us in connection with some of the Beethoven quartets, and
like numbers of Russian proprietors who have never
been heard of out of their own country, maintained
a private orchestra, composed of serfs specially
educated in music.   The education of the serf
musicians was sometimes superintended by the proprietor himself, who, if he happened to be a composer, enjoyed admirable opportunities for getting
his works executed.   After working with and for
his relative's orchestra as a youth, Glinka entered
the Corps of Engineers, and remained in it a sufficient time to stamp him as a willing servant of the
State.   Then he left the army and went first to
Milan, then to Berlin, to pursue his musical studies
in a systematic manner.

The opera of *Zisn Za Tsarya*, or, *Life for the Tsar*,
in which Glinka's Tsar-rejected composition now
figures, and to the score of which it may possibly
have belonged when presented for the great National
Anthem competition as an independent piece, was
produced at Moscow in 1843; and since that year it
has been played so often that the melodies, for the
most part of Russian type, in which it abounds are

familiar to all Russia. Luckily for the success of
the work it is based on a story which appeals at
once to the patriotism and the loyalty of the public.
Nor is there anything in this loyalty which could
shock even a Nihilist, unless, indeed, the Nihilism of
the unhappy man were of so comprehensive a character as to leave him nothing in the way of heart.
The plot of the piece, which was written by Count
Rosen, turns upon the devotion of a peasant named
Ivan Soussanin, who sacrificed his life to ensure
the safety of the Tsar Michael. The action, as
before mentioned, takes place at the time of the
occupation of Moscow by the Poles, just two centuries and three-quarters ago. In the first act the
miserable condition of Russia is set forth; also the
affection of the peasant hero, the aforesaid "Ivan
Soussanin," for his family, which yields only in
intensity to his love for the Tsar. This particular Tsar is a worthy object of devotion, for he
thinks only of the liberation of his country from the
dominion of the hated Poles, and meanwhile is in a
position of danger and distress. He is even a fugitive in the woods, and here the sturdy "Ivan Soussanin" will, in the last act, be ordered by the Poles
to find him.

The whole of the second act is occupied with an
exhibition of Polish festivities at Moscow. To the
Russians throughout the opera homeliness, combined

with honesty, is attributed; while the Poles are represented as brilliant and warlike, but at the same time light-hearted and frivolous. To judge by their demeanour in Glinka's work they do nothing when the battle is once at an end but drink, dance, and enjoy themselves. The whole, indeed, of the second or Polish act consists of ballet-music in the national Polish style. A lively, highly-rhythmical mazurka, with a great number of themes and constant contrasts of instrumentation, is followed by a stately but very brilliant polonaise, which in turn is succeeded by an animated krakoviak; and the suite of dances is, if I remember rightly, brought to a conclusion by some sort of coda. The mazurka is especially popular with the Russians, who trouble themselves no more about its Polish origin than we in England do about the possibly anti-English origin of an Irish ballad; and the opening phrase of the mazurka is used in " leading motive " fashion whenever in the third act there is any question of the Poles or their doings. Glinka, by the way, has made a more remarkable use of this device in his *Ruslan and Ludmila,* where the bad character, " Tchernomor," is persistently accompanied by a hideous descending scale consisting entirely of whole tones. In the third act of *Zisn Za Tsarya* we have to deal with a wood; a snowstorm; " Ivan Soussanin," who has taken farewell of his much-

loved family that he may devote himself to his
country's liberation; and a band of Polish soldiers
under one of their highly-military, mazurka-dancing
officers. The Poles are in pursuit of the unhappy
Tsar, who has taken flight, and is supposed to be
somewhere in the forest. " Ivan Soussanin" is
seized, and, in accordance with the laws of war
(though in disregard of those of humanity), is ordered
to act as guide and lead the Polish troops to the
Tsar's place of concealment. "Ivan Soussanin"
is, in his ordinary mood, light-hearted and jocular.
He possesses, moreover, a taste for practical
jokes. Instead, then, of making any objections to
the task imposed upon him by his country's
oppressors, he declares himself quite ready to execute it, and, telling the Poles to follow him, leads
them merrily into the thicket until at last, more and
more involved in the hopeless labyrinth and half-
frozen by the cold (for there is a pitiless wind and
the snow is still falling), they adopt a stern tone
towards Ivan and ask him whether he has been
trifling with them. The patriotic peasant asks in
return whether they really supposed him capable of
betraying his Sovereign into the hands of his enemies,
and then, exposing his breast to their swords, sings
to them to do their worst, and singing dies.

The curtain falls on the group formed by " Ivan
Soussanin" defying the Poles and the Poles preparing

to strike him.   In the epilogue we see the Soussanin family regretting the heroic Ivan, but in no whining spirit.   He has died for his country and his Tsar.   A monument, seen on the stage, has been erected to his memory; and the Prince whose life he saved now enters Moscow amid the applause of his subjects and at the head of his troops.

CHAPTER III.

THE question whether England is or is not a musical nation has been discussed often enough, and would have been settled long ago if anything in this world could be settled by mere argument. But as the expression, "musical nation," can be understood in several different senses, and as disputants seldom take the trouble to explain what their propositions are really intended to signify, it is probable that the controversy as to whether and to what extent England may be considered a musical nation will be continued for many a long year. Meanwhile, those who wish to arrive at the truth in connection with this matter, will do well to remember that "musical nation" is a description which may be fitly applied to a nation which gives birth to great composers, great singers, and great instrumental musicians, but which is not equally suited to a nation which enjoys

and appreciates good music without producing much
of it in any form. The music executed in the
principal concert-rooms and at the principal opera-
houses of Europe is almost always the work of
Italian, German, or French composers; and in the
list of singers and instrumental musicians whose
fame extends over the whole civilized world, the
names of but few Englishmen or Englishwomen will
be found. It has been held that music thrives only
where the grape ripens, and there is much truth in
the theory so far as the cultivation of the art from
the composer's and singer's point of view is concerned. But as wine may be thoroughly enjoyed in
lands where, out of hothouses, there are no vines,
so music may be fully appreciated in countries where
great composers are rare phenomena, and where
music, though not absolutely wanting as a national
product, yet never attains the importance of an article
of export. There is no kind of music worth hearing
which, sooner or later, does not get heard in England; and there are no musical artists of true merit
who, whatever their origin, cannot count upon receiving in England unbounded and permanent hospitality. The list of foreign composers who, from
the time of Handel to that of Sir Julius Benedict,
have settled in England would be a long one; and
it would be interminable if to this list were added the
names of those who have visited this country for a

time and have written works specially for production at our opera-houses and concert-rooms. But
the most remarkable document of the kind would
be a catalogue of all the eminent singers who, during
the last century and a half or more, have accepted
engagements in England. It would be seen that,
since the first introduction of the comparatively
modern entertainment called Opera, every vocalist
of European celebrity has, during some portion of
his or her career, sung in London ; while no incon-
siderable number of distinguished foreign artists
have made London their home.

No one of the great *prime donne*, however,
became so thoroughly . English as Mademoiselle
Titiens at the time of her lamented death had
become. The late Madame Grisi ended by settling
in London; but during the first part of her career
she belonged as much to France as to England, and
more to Italy, the land of her birth, than to either
of the two countries which she turn by turn adopted.
A great portion, too, of Madame Adelina Patti's life
has been spent in England ; and London is the only
capital in which that admirable artist has sung
season after season, without one break, for a period
of seventeen years. Mdlle. Titiens, however, made
her first appearance in London two years earlier than
Madame Adelina Patti, and for nearly twenty years
she lived almost exclusively in England. During

the whole of that time Mdlle. Titiens sang every season at Her Majesty's Theatre, or " Her Majesty's Opera," as the establishment was called, when, for a certain number of years, it was located at Drury Lane. Every autumn her services were in request for our provincial festivals, and the very year of her death she was engaged for the two great triennial musical celebrations of Gloucester and of Leeds.

A certain number of operatic characters may be said to die with Mdlle. Titiens. For a time, at least, it will be very difficult to find a " Norma " or a " Lucrezia Borgia ; " while it will be impossible to meet with a perfect representative of " Donna Anna " or of " Fidelio." Years hence, when a new impersonation of Mozart's or of Beethoven's heroine is attempted, the candidate for the highest honours of lyric art will be tried by the standard of the great dramatic singer whose loss we still deplore. Not to suffer in such parts as those just named, by comparison with Mdlle. Titiens, will be an advantage reserved for those who must indeed be pronounced incomparable. Nor will it be by her artistic merits alone that Mdlle. Titiens will be remembered. The qualities that go towards the making up of a really great prima donna are many and varied. Besides a fine and powerful voice, a perfect style, and high dramatic ability, she must possess great physical strength and that particular kind of force, half

physical, half moral, which is known by the name of
" nerve." This species of courage enabled Mdlle.
Titiens to do her duty, and more than her duty to
the public, at times when many a vocalist, of perhaps
equal merit in a purely artistic point of view, would
have given way. Like other singers, Mdlle. Titiens
must have been now and then indisposed, and from
time to time seriously unwell. But when was an
excuse ever put forward on her behalf? The first
time that, after having been announced to sing, she
found herself absolutely unable to appear, she was
already suffering from the incurable malady which a
few months later was to carry her off. It savours of
presumption to speculate as to whether the end of
any human being might or might not have been
happier. But as regards Mdlle. Titiens's artistic
fame, it is scarcely to be regretted that she should
have died at a time when her reputation was at
its highest. She continued singing, not, indeed, until
her death, but until the moment had arrived for the
first of a series of terrible operations to be performed,
of which the immediate effect was naturally to in-
capacitate her for appearing on the stage. Opera-
goers know well that Mdlle. Titiens was never more
expressive as a singer, never more impressive as an
actress, than at the beginning of the season which
was to prove her last It had already been
made known to her that she was in a dangerous

condition and that she must place herself in the hands of a surgeon. But she was determined not to give up her active career until she should be absolutely forced to do so; and she sang through an entire evening, and sang with her invariable success, well knowing that on the fall of the curtain she was to take farewell of her ideal existence as an operatic heroine, to lead—certainly for some considerable time, probably until the end of her days—the life of a suffering invalid. But, true heroine that she was, she persevered at her appointed duties until she was suddenly incapacitated by a wound she knew beforehand she was to receive. What high faculties of endurance and of self-concentration she must have possessed to be able thus, at the very last moment, to forget what threatened her in her very existence in order to devote herself entirely to her work as an artist! Her courage will long be spoken of by those who happen to have known something of the closing period of her life, though it will be by her artistic qualities, and by her love for the noblest creations of the lyric stage, that she will be known to posterity.

Mendel, in his "Musical Lexicon," speaks of Mdlle. Titiens as "the celebrated prima donna of Her Majesty's Theatre;" and, in fact, with the exception of one season, that of 1869, when she sang at the Royal Italian Opera as principal dramatic soprano of the combined company, jointly directed

by Messrs. Gye and Mapleson, Mdlle. Titiens sang
at Her Majesty's Theatre from 1859, the year of
her first appearance in London, until 1877, the year
of her death. Born at Hamburgh in 1831 of Hungarian parents (her real name was Tietjens), she
came out in her native city, at the age of 18, as
" Lucrezia Borgia," one of her most famous parts.
From Hamburgh she went to Frankfort, at that
time the capital of the Germanic Confederation; and
from Frankfort to Vienna, where she particularly
distinguished herself by her truly admirable impersonation of " Valentine" in *Les Huguenots.* In
oratorio Mdlle. Titiens sang as finely as in opera;
and she had not been many months in England
when engagements were offered to her at our great
provincial festivals.

Mdlle. Titiens sang the part of " Ortrud" in
Lohengrin so finely that we may safely say that
she would have sung Wagner's music generally as
well as she sang that of Rossini, Donizetti, and
Meyerbeer, of Mozart, Beethoven, and Weber. But
she was never heard in any Wagnerian part except
that of " Ortrud." With the Wagnerian movement,
which lasted in England for some years, she had
little to do. When, indeed, Mdlle. Ilma de Murska
had appeared as " Senta," and Madame Albani as
" Elsa " and as " Elizabeth," and Madame Nilsson
and Mdlle. Titiens in the same cast as " Elsa " and

as " Ortrud," then the work of propagandism was taken up by German companies; and it is to them alone that we are indebted for the representations given in London of the *Meister singer* and of the *Ring des Nibelungen.*

It did not happen *cuivis homini* to visit Bayreuth in the great days when that honoured town was making holiday, and when at certain solemn hours of the day trumpeters, as if in imitation of the warders in the second act of *Lohengrin,* sounded the more or less cheerful horn in token of the memorable fact that the performances were about to begin.

But of those who claim to be reckoned among the initiated, few would assert that the cycle of Bayreuth is to any single work of the same composer, what in Tennyson's phrase, " A cycle of Cathay," is to the briefest period of European civilization. " Cyclus," however, was for a time a name to conjure with; and, should the fashion last, we may expect operatic managers to extend the application of the magic word in various directions. A Mozart cyclus, for instance, made up of such familiar works as the *Marriage of Figaro, Don Giovanni,* and the *Magic Flute,* would possess considerable interest for well-meaning persons whose capacity for appreciating the higher manifestations of the composer's art has not been

sufficiently developed. Cyclus, however, is a designation which at present is exclusively reserved
for Wagnerian use. At Her Majesty's Theatre one
Wagnerian cycle followed another, until at last no
fewer than four complete cycles had been counted.
Nobody was allowed to subscribe for less than one
perfect cycle; and it was rumoured that the title of
"bicyclist" would be conferred on those who went
through two cycles; of "tricyclist" on those who
sat out three, and so on. Whatever may be
thought of Herr Wagner as a poet, a composer,
and a critic—and he has distinguished himself
equally in these three characters—there can be no
question as to his fertility in ideas, and in ideas
which are themselves reproductive. The father of
some of the most remarkable operatic works ever
produced, he is, so to say, the grandfather of a host
of critical and descriptive books which those works,
and especially the "cycle" of operas on the subject
of the *Nibelung's Ring*, have inspired. There is a
constantly increasing Wagner literature as there is
a literature of Goethe and of Shakespeare.

Indeed, in London, as in other capitals, the
number of publications in one form or another
called forth by Herr Wagner's works is considerable. The *Nibelungen Ring* alone has given birth
to some half dozen, including a translation of the
poem, in imitative alliterative verse, by Mr. For-

man; a more literal translation, on the principle of
"words to music," by Mr. Corder; a somewhat
labyrinthine guide to the music of the *Nibelung's
Ring*, by Herr von Wolzogen, and a very complete
account of the poem, the music, and the representation, as it took place at Bayrenth in 1876, by Mr.
Jackson, well known through his excellent translations of several of Herr Wagner's operas. Without the slightest disrespect to Herr von Wolzogen,
who is evidently a man of " light and leading," it
may be hoped, in the interests of amateurs bent on
studying and comprehending the *Ring*, that a
guide to his guide will some day be brought
out; though, should its publication be too long
delayed, the *Ring* itself, with its marvellous
incidents and its miraculous intricacies, may
possibly be forgotten. Meanwhile the spirit of the
poem can best be seized through Mr. Forman's
really admirable translation, executed in a metrical
form which corresponds closely to that of the
original; while for the thorough understanding of
the music, Mr. Corder's word and note translations,
and Herr von Wolzogen's well intended but somewhat too mysterious guide, may be found valuable. To enjoy the *Ring of the Nibelung* in the
fullest possible manner it would be desirable to
bring to the representation an intimate knowledge
of the subject, a certain familiarity with the

peculiarities of the Wagnerian metrical system, and at least a tolerable acquaintance with the " leading motives," to the number of ninety, which indicate the personality of the principal characters, or are associated with the manifestation of a particular sentiment or passion, or which in some cases emphasize the occurrence of essential and carefully prepared incidents. The task may frighten the mere lover of music, but to the devoted student it is not altogether impossible.

CHAPTER IV.

PATTI.

MADAME ADELINA PATTI, being one of the celebrities of the century, has been made the subject of many biographies. None is so likely to be correct as the one given in fragments by her brother-in-law, the late Maurice Strakosch, in various chapters of his " Souvenirs d'un Impresario." The illustrious Adelina was, according to Mr. Strakosch, born on the operatic stage, or nearly so. Her mother, a famous prima donna, was playing the part of " Norma " at Madrid, when suddenly, as the curtain was about to rise for the last act, she was taken ill. She was driven home, and soon afterwards Adelina made positively the first of all her first appearances. Incredible as it may seem (although those who have heard little Josef Hofmann will be in a position to believe it), Adelina Patti was able to sing all kinds of operatic airs when she was only six years of age.

She had, it is true, heard them sung by artists who were likely enough to make a deep impression on a sensitive musical nature : Jenny Lind, for instance, Grisi, Bosio, Sontag, Alboni, Frezzolini, Piccolomini, and Parepa-Rosa.

It has been said that Adelina Patti's mother was herself a famous singer. It was under the name of Barilli that she obtained her earliest triumphs. Then she married Salvatore Patti, an impresario, whose operatic speculations led him to all parts of the world. Madame Barilli was a member of his company. Her first husband was a composer of distinction.

Adelina Patti, then, sometimes spoken of as an American, is, in fact, Italian by both parents ; nor, it has been seen, was she even born in America. Her father, however, took her to the United States when she was only three years old, so that she was really brought up under American influences, including the influence of the American climate; a favourable one, without doubt, for the singing voice. Adelina received her first lessons in reading, writing, pianoforte playing, and singing from a friend of the family, Madame Paravelli; and it was to Madame Paravelli's accompaniment that the little girl sang her first operatic airs. Maurice Strakosch, good pianist, excellent singing-master (he had studied with Madame Pasta) and tenor in his early days at

£4 a month, had made the acquaintance of Salvatore Patti at Vicenza in 1843. In 1848, at the time of the February Revolution, which replaced the rule of Louis Philippe by that of the second Republic, Maurice Strakosch was at Paris. In the midst of the political excitement he saw no chance of prosperity for operatic affairs; so, abandoning the old world for the new, he arrived suddenly at New York, where he found his old friend Salvatore Patti endeavouring, but in vain, to inspire the Americans of that day with a taste for Italian music. Up to this time Italian Opera had met with but little success in the United States, which may, in some degree, have been the fault, not of the Americans, but of the Italians. No complete company of Italian singers had as yet come before the American public. The famous one directed by Garcia must have possessed many points of attraction, since it included Malibran and other members of the Garcia family among its members. America, however, was not at that time the " promised land " of opera singers. Nor does it appear that in the year 1848 Salvatore Patti had in his company any vocalists of European reputation such as alone would have been likely to draw the American public.

Strakosch had not been long in the United States when he was engaged to arrange the musical performances for a festival which was to be given at

New York on the 2nd October, 1848. He began by securing the services of the Salvatore Patti company, and after the festival, which was thoroughly successful, he signed a contract with Mdlle. Amalia Patti, Adelina's elder sister. Mdlle. Amalia Patti and Mdlle. Parodi, Pasta's eminent pupil, were at that time the favourite singers of the American public; and Strakosch engaged both of them for a tour through the United States, at the end of which he made Mdlle. Amalia Patti his wife.

According to the author of the " Souvenirs d'un Impresario," Adelina Patti was in 1848 six years of age. The same writer tells us that in 1850 (no month named) she was eight years of age; whence it must be concluded that she was born some time in 1842 ; though according to Grove's " Musical Dictionary," February 19th, 1843, was her birthday. Adelina Patti, except perhaps in her girlhood, has never looked her age ; but Maurice Strakosch gives his dates with an air of certainty, however fantastic they may seem.

Salvatore Patti had been replaced as manager of the Italian Opera at New York by Max Maretzek, orchestral conductor and composer of ballet music, known at one time in London by a pretty and striking waltz which he had written for a company of juvenile dancers from Vienna who appeared with success some forty years ago at Her Majesty's

Theatre. In 1850 Mr. Maretzek engaged little Adelina Patti, then eight years of age, and introduced her to the public at a charity concert. On this interesting occasion the little girl, who eleven years afterwards was to be recognized as the most brilliant vocalist in Europe, sang the final rondo of *La Sonnambula* and the " Echo Song," first made popular by Jenny Lind. The sensation she produced was immense; and the morning after the concert she was already celebrated.

From the age of eight to that of eleven Adelina Patti travelled with Strakosch, who began at Baltimore a series of concerts in which she was to take part. In spite of the fame she enjoyed at New York, her reputation had not reached Baltimore; for at the opening of the concert —though the price of admission was but a half-dollar to all parts of the hall—only 100 persons took tickets. At the second 300 persons were present; while at the third the hall was quite full, 2,000 tickets having been sold.

At Baltimore Strakosch fell in with Ole Bull, the famous Norwegian violinist, who on his first appearance in England was hailed as another Paganini, though on returning to this country many years later a more reasonable view was taken of his talent—more showy than solid. Ole Bull, however, performed wonderful feats on his instrument, and his name was a great attraction in a concert programme. Accordingly, Strakosch enlisted his services, and the leading, if not the sole members of the Strakosch Concert Company were now Adelina Patti and Ole Bull.

In her childhood Adelina Patti was capricious; a peculiarity which, in maturer years, operatic vocalists are said never to exhibit. She liked singing; but she also took pleasure in the society of other children, and she was fond of dolls. It can be readily believed that the little vocalist of eight years did not care much for exercises and scales, and it was sometimes difficult to make her give up the games of her age when the time had come for her to go through her daily studies. These, thanks to Strakosch, were never altogether neglected, though ingenuity was sometimes shown in evading them. One day, at Cincinnati, the child of genius had asked Strakosch for a doll. The impresario, his mind intent on higher things, had forgotten the request. He had, however, promised a doll, and promises of this kind are not forgotten by the children to whom they have been made. Accordingly, when the time came for Adelina to sing at the concert she reminded her brother-in-law that she had not yet received her doll. The hall was already full, and Strakosch did his best to make the young artist sing first, and talk about the doll afterwards.

But she was inflexible; and it was not until after Strakosch had gone out and bought her the required doll that she consented to ascend the platform. Then, full of joy as a minute before of grief, she sang delightfully, and the audience applauded with enthusiasm.

With a passion for dolls Adelina Patti combined a taste for champagne. Sitting next her at dinner, Ole Bull neglected or refused to give her a glass of her favourite wine; "on which," says Maurice Strakosch, "the little girl in her indignation administered to the famous violinist a vigorous slap."

With commendable prudence Strakosch had recommended that from the age of twelve to that of fifteen Mdlle. Patti should not sing in public, a period of repose seeming necessary in order to allow her beautiful voice to develop itself without any risk of being strained.

While, however, Strakosch was engaged in composing an opera called *John of Naples*, which was produced at New York in 1857, with Mdlle. Parodi in the principal part, the celebrated Gottschalk prevailed upon Adelina's parents to allow him to take her on a tour through India.

In 1859 Strakosch became director of the Italian Opera at New York, and here, "at the age of sixteen," he says, "Adelina Patti made her first appearance on any stage."

" She was already at that time the charming woman and the adorable artist that she is now."

It was on the 24th of November that this interesting *début* took place, and if, as Maurice Strakosch tells us, the youthful Adelina was at that time only sixteen, it follows that, contrary to his previous statement, she must have been born in 1843. With a neglect which it is difficult to forgive, Strakosch, so prodigal of less important details, fails to mention the opera in which Adelina Patti sang " for the first time on any stage." Muzio, now chiefly known as one of Verdi's most intimate friends, conducted the orchestra on the evening of the famous first appearance; and in the course of the season the new prima donna sang with immense success in *The Barber of Seville*, *La Sonnambula*, *Don Pasquale*, *I Puritani*, *Martha*, *Don Giovanni*, *La Traviata*, *Il Trovatore*, *Rigoletto*, *Ernani*, *Mosè in Egitto*, and *Linda di Chamouni*. In all of these, with the exception of *Mosè in Egitto*, Madame Patti has sung with the most brilliant success in London, where to her juvenile repertory, in itself sufficiently extensive, she has added some twenty or thirty other works.

After his sister-in-law's immense success Strakosch tore up the contract by which she was bound to sing for him during five years, on comparatively moderate terms. By the terms of this agreement Adelina Patti was to receive for the first year 2,000, for the second 3,000, for the third 4,000, for the fourth and fifth 5,000 francs a month. " Contrast this," says Strakosch, " with what Madame Patti received a few years ago at San Francisco, where Mr. Mapleson paid her £1,000 for each performance." Strakosch now signed a new contract, which, he tells us, was acted upon as long as his business relations with Madame Patti were continued, and by the terms of which singer and impresario were, after payment of general expenses, to share profits.

Offers of an engagement were now received from every side. " North America, South America, Mexico, were all," says Strakosch, " disputing for Adelina Patti, whose renown in the new world was now greater than ever." She was on her way to Mexico, where the public awaited her with the greatest impatience, when an unexpected incident occurred. In the St. Louis Hotel, at New Orleans, two young ladies told her that they had just arrived from Mexico, where they had been attacked, robbed, and frightfully maltreated by brigands. This was enough to determine the young prima donna not to continue her journey. Nothing could induce her to change her decision, and after a visit to Havana she embarked for England, where an engagement had been offered to her at Her Majesty's Theatre. The manager of that historical Opera-house was just then Mr. E. T. Smith, a gentleman who afterwards "ran" an "Italian Opera for the People" at Drury Lane; it having occurred to him, as he informed the public at the end of one of his operatic representations, that this class of entertainment had too long been given exclusively for the benefit of " My Lord Tomnoddy." Mr. E. T. Smith was an impresario of quite a new kind. Ignorant not only of music (in which there would be nothing novel), but of the authorship of the most popular operas, he once in a public programme attributed *Don Giovanni* to Verdi; and he is said to have found it difficult to distinguish "*La Traviatore*" from "*Il Troviata.*" Mr. Smith knew, however, that Adelina Patti had made a great success in America, and he offered her £400 per month to sing in London. Just at that time Mr. Frederick Gye, annoyed at the existence of two Italian operas when one would have been quite enough, offered Mr. Smith £4,000 not to open. Mr. E. T. Smith, preferring certain gain to probable loss, accepted the offer; and when Maurice Strakosch arrived in London with Salvatore Patti and his charming daughter he found Her Majesty's Theatre closed.

Maurice Strakosch had now the proverbial two courses open to him—either to bring an action against Mr. E. T. Smith, which would in no way benefit his sister-in-law as an artist; or apply for an engagement to Mr. Gye. He, of course, applied to Mr. Gye, who, however, already had so many distinguished singers in his company that he did not wish to increase the number. Several new vocalists had, moreover, during the last few years appeared at the Royal Italian Opera without success; and the manager was not inclined to make any fresh experiments with *débutantes*. Maurice Strakosch, however, was not the man to be put off with refusals, which in this case were without basis ; for, whatever number of great vocalists might be already included in Mr. Gye's company, and however many newcomers might, of late years, have failed, he knew well that Adelina Patti would not fail, and that no company, however rich in talent, could afford to dispense with her services.

If Mr. Gye would agree to nothing else, he might, at least, said Strakosch, give the young girl a trial. To this Mr. Gye, knowing Strakosch to be a man of the soundest judgment in musical matters, could not but consent. Strakosch stipulated, prudently enough, that Adelina should have three trial performances ; since it was always possible that at the first, perhaps even the second, she would not be fully mistress of her resources. These trial performances were to be given gratuitously ; but it was arranged that in case of success Adelina Patti should be engaged at the rate of £150 a month for the first year, £200 for the second, £250 for the third, £300 for the fourth, and £400 for the fifth. The engagement was to be signed before the first trial performance, and it was only to be valid in the event of Mr. Gye feeling satisfied. It was further agreed that Mdlle. Patti should sing twice a week.

I had been accustomed for several years previously, except for a few long intervals spent in France, Germany, or Russia, to attend all important operatic performances, especially on the occasion of a first appearance, or the production of a new work. But the first appearances during the two or three previous seasons had not been encouraging; and when that appearance of Adelina Patti was announced, I remember saying to myself that this *début* would probably be like several others that of late years I had witnessed. I intended to start the same evening for Warsaw, where troubles had begun, which, two years later, were to culminate in an insurrection; and though my instructions were to get to the scene of action as rapidly as possible, I might have deferred my departure until the next morning and still have reached my destination without any appreciable loss of time.

In those days the Dover Express left Charing Cross at 8.30, and I afterwards calculated that when Adelina Patti first appeared on the stage of the Royal Italian Opera, and began to sing the recitative of Amina's " cavatina " in *La Sonnambula*, I must have been somewhere near Croydon. I certainly, however, was not thinking at the time of Adelina Patti, whose name I had probably already forgotten, but rather of Polish affairs, and how I should be received when I made my own " first appearance " at Warsaw, now in a state of siege.

Some six or seven months later, after spending some time in the " Kingdom " and other parts of Poland, I was on my way to St. Petersburg, when at Kovno, in Lithuania, where at that time travellers coming from Prussia had to get their passports *viséd* and their luggage examined before proceeding by diligence to St. Petersburg, I heard a voice, which I fancied I recognized, lifted up as if in a spirit of contention —

" Does it hurt your hand much, scribbling away incessantly in that style ? " asked in the French language the proprietor, or rather proprietress, of the voice.

" So, so. Not particularly," replied, in an imitation of French, the person who had been addressed.

" I am sorry for it," said the lady, half to herself.

I entered the half diligence, half passport-office, where this conversation was going on, and found that the more fluent of the two speakers was the charming mezzo-soprano, Madame Nantier Didiée.

She was on her way to St. Petersburg with a number of other singers, all engaged at the Imperial Opera-house; and after her long journey from London was much irritated, she said (though she seemed, above all, amused), at the petty worries inflicted upon her by the passport official, who wanted to know everything, and seemed himself to know nothing.

She had never before in her life seen such a horrible place as Kovno. And then it was so cold. The winter had now begun, and the ground was covered with snow. I prevailed upon her to take a short walk round the town, of which I remember very little, except that on a commemorative pillar this laconic inscription was to be read :

" In 1812 an army of all nations passed through this town 700,000 strong. In 1813 it returned 70,000 strong : "

An inscription as good, in its way, as the one cut on the Borodino monument, which runs thus :

" Napoleon, Moscow, 1812; Alexander, Paris, 1814."

Madame Nantier Didiée hated politics ; but she wanted to know when we got back to the diligence-office, which was at the same time a Government bureau and an inn, what one of the functionaries meant by telling us that as it was now dark we must not go out again without a lantern.

" What do they mean ? Are there mad dogs in the place ? " she inquired of the functionary ; the same who had *viséd* her passport, and who now began again to make entries in some book.

" There are no mad dogs," said a Polish gentleman, who now came up ; " they are afraid of ghosts. This is a corner of ancient Poland."

" With these men perpetually scribbling, and such a number of fleas," replied Madame Nantier Didiée, " it is not astonishing that the Poles rise in insurrection."

I secured a place in the same diligence—they used to run in caravans of two or three, according to the number of passengers—and Madame Nantier Didiée enlivened the long journey to St. Petersburg by telling me what had taken place in London during the season that I had missed.

" No one," she said, " paid the least attention to any of *us*. We are all crushed by that little Patti."

" Who," I asked, " is ' that little Patti ? ' " For I thought I had never heard of her, though, on reflection, I remembered that this was the name of the vocalist whose first appearance I had missed.

" You must have been living in the desert," exclaimed the vivacious mezzo-soprano. " But you said you had been in Poland ; it's the same thing. Adelina Patti is a young artist with a light soprano voice, brilliant execution, and engaging manners, who has driven the London public absolutely wild. Nothing but Patti goes down with them now."

She added that she had sung with the new prima donna in *Martha*, and that in spite of the overpowering success gained by the frolicsome " Lady Henrietta," the audience had still some plaudits to bestow on her not very staid friend " Lady Nancy": the part, it need scarcely be added, which Madame Nantier Didiée used to fill with so much talent and grace.

" What," I asked, " did Davison think of her ? "

Davison, I was told, admired her more than anyone else, and was most enthusiastic in her praise.

He had appreciated her, indeed, from the first; witness his article on the young *débutante* in the *Times* of May 15th, 1861.

It was not until 1862 that I heard Madame Patti. I at once found what I knew would prove to be the case, that Madame Nantier Didiée had given me a perfectly just account of the wonderful vocalist. She was, indeed, charming ; alike admirable in expressive music and in the music of display ; full of brilliancy, full of feeling; singing on all occasions and in every style so spontaneously that her natural language seemed to be not speech, but song.

To have the services of such a singer as Madame Adelina Patti for five years, at a rising salary of from £150 to £400 a month, was indeed a piece of good fortune for the manager. It will be remembered that Madame Patti was only bound by her engagement to sing twice a week for Mr. Gye. If she sang a third night he agreed to pay her on each occasion £100; and Maurice Strakosch assures us that until her marriage with the Marquis de Caux she never received more than £120 a night. Of late years Madame Patti is known to have received from Mr. Mapleson £500, £600, and in America as much as £1,000 a night. At the earlier figures she was as sure to enrich her manager as at the later ones to ruin him.

After her first season in London Mdlle. Patti went to Brussels, where she met with as much success from the public as in London, though with less from the critics. One Belgian newspaper, while admitting her talent, is said to have recommended the young artist to continue her studies for a time at the Brussels Conservatoire.

From Brussels the new singer, who was gradually making for herself a European reputation, went on to Berlin, where Pauline Lucca was the favourite of the day. Mdlle. Lucca was about the same age as her rival, who had come to challenge her on her own ground; and, says Maurice Strakosch, " she was equally pretty." The director of the Royal Theatre found himself, after engaging Mdlle. Patti, in this strange position. He possessed in his com-

pany two admirable singers; but while he paid
Mdlle. Lucca 1,000 francs a month, Mdlle. Patti
was to receive 1,000 francs a night. Accordingly
for the simplest commercial reasons he must have
been more anxious that Mdlle. Lucca should eclipse
Mdlle. Patti than that Mdlle. Patti should eclipse
Mdlle. Lucca.

On arriving at Berlin Mdlle. Patti, as a stranger
and as the last comer, hastened to pay Mdlle. Lucca
a visit. Mdlle. Lucca lived at this time on a
fourth floor (though the loftiness of one's abode has
not so much significance in Continental capitals as
in London), and she received her visitors—Maurice
Strakosch and his sister-in-law—not only in her
bedroom, but in bed. "Between the sheets,"
writes Strakosch, " she looked like a child ; and
with her first words she expressed her astonishment
at seeing Adelina Patti, who, like herself, was a
delicate and adorable little creature. 'What ! '
repeated Lucca, as if in spite of herself, ' are you
the great Patti ?' No rivalry existed between the
two singers except on the stage. Away from the
theatre they remained on the most friendly terms.
In spite of the Press, which showed itself hostile,
Adelina Patti triumphed with the public ; and King
William, who was not yet Emperor, attended all her
performances, and went to congratulate her in her
box."

At Amsterdam and at The Hague, Mdlle. Patti met with the same success. The King of Holland, as much subjugated by her beautiful voice as any of his people, invited her to sing at the Palace. Merelli, director of the Italian Company at The Hague, replied to the Chamberlain charged with the negotiations that Patti could not sing for less than 3,000 francs a night. The price seemed enormous, and the Chamberlain asked for time to consider. " *On assure*," says Strakosch, without saying to whom the assurance was given, "that the Dutch Cabinet assembled on this occasion, and that it was not until after a Ministerial decision had been pronounced that the King consented to Merelli's terms."

It now seemed to be the turn of Paris to receive a visit from Mdlle. Patti. M. Calzado objected to pay £50 a night—the sum asked by Strakosch. These terms, however, were accepted by him the year afterwards, with an increase of £10 a night for the next season but one. Under the management of M. Bagier, by whom M. Calzado was succeeded, Patti received 2,000 francs a performance for the first year, 2,500 for the second, and 3,000 for the third; and Strakosch declares that in his time this last figure was never exceeded. On such terms as these Italian Opera may be carried on with some prospect of success; and 3,000 francs

a night is, after all, good pay. But enough of
pounds, shillings, and pence, except to point out
once more—what Maurice Strakosch emphasizes
again and again in his interesting book—that the
ridiculous payments now made to operatic stars
are the ruin alike of operatic management and
operatic art. The prima donna herself suffers
when she is feebly supported by worn-out tenors,
baritones who have never learned to sing, and
incapable vocalists of all kinds. But what
others can a manager engage when nearly the
whole of his estimated profits are swallowed up by
one voracious artist, whose thoughts are not of art,
but of gold ? A great prima donna has, of
course, as much right as a great painter or a great
poet to fix her own terms. But the painter and
the poet are self-dependent, whereas the singer
depends for success in a great measure on the
singing of associates ; and no person of ordinary
musical taste can care for an operatic representation
in which one singer is as admirable as, under the
circumstances, she can be, while the others are
quite incompetent.

In all probability it will prove useless now, as
heretofore, to lecture on this subject. Rachel,
Ristori, Sarah Bernhardt have all been guilty of
the fault charged against Madame Patti, and which
in the early part of the century used to be charged

against Madame Catalani. But an artist, however
great, who consents to perform in the midst of
inadequate supporters ceases to be anything more
than a highly interesting curiosity, or, let us say,
phenomenon.

Already in London, as in other great capitals,
the public refuses to be attracted by such exhibi-
tions ; and it is only in outlandish countries that
the " star," operatic or dramatic, can hope for the
golden harvest reaped at the cost of much that
does not deserve to be cut down.

Madame Patti has been so much flattered, and
has obtained such brilliant triumphs, that she may,
perhaps, be excused for believing that every operatic
representation in which she takes part derives
interest from her singing alone. Three times,
however, she has tested this principle in operas of
her own choice, by Signor Campana, Prince Ponia-
towski, and M. Lenepveu ; and though in each
work the whole interest was concentrated in the part
assigned to Madame Patti, neither "Esmeralda," nor
" Gelmina," nor " Velléda " obtained the slightest
success.

Adelina Patti was as yet far from having reached
the thousand-pound-a-night period of her career.
When she sang in Vienna, at the beginning of 1863,
she was receiving one thousand pounds a month :
so Mr. Strakosch told me at the time. Towards the

end of February, 1863, I was again on my way to
Poland, which from a state of agitation had passed
to one of open insurrection; and having a few
hours to spare at Vienna I turned them to profit-
able account by going to see Adelina Patti in
the part of "Norina." I had been told on her
own authority that she played it, not as in London, where Costa would allow no upsetting
of furniture, no vigorous slaps in the face, administered to "Don Pasquale" by his insubordinate
ward, his rebellious bride; but with an impulsiveness
and a self-abandonment which she herself thought
natural in the character, and which she, in any case,
practised—to the entire satisfaction, it must be
added, of the Viennese public. Never, indeed, did
I see the charming vocalist and actress play with so
much gaiety, so much vivacity, so thoroughly in the
spirit of Italian comedy, as on this one occasion at
Vienna.

I was afterwards told by a Hungarian friend
who greatly admired Mdlle. Patti, and had vainly
endeavoured to get introduced to her at Vienna—
though, with that view, he had attended many evening parties to which she had been invited—that the
Viennese found her by no means sociable. How,
indeed, was the young artist to accept the hospitality
offered to her in every direction and yet preserve
enough health and spirits to support the excitement

of three performances a week, which she was now giving; performances, moreover, into which she threw herself heart and soul, with all the energy of her impetuous nature?

Strakosch was accused, much to his credit, of saving her from all such trouble and fatigue as could well be avoided; and the Viennese attributed to the influence of her brother-in-law the persistence of Adelina Patti in refusing their invitations. With a view of sparing Adelina all unnecessary efforts, Strakosch not only attended to all her business affairs, but replaced her now and then at rehearsals. Thanks to a prodigious memory, Madame Patti is able in a great measure to dispense with rehearsals, and according to M. Guy de Charnacé (see Adelina Patti in " Les Etoiles du Chant ") Mr. Strakosch has often on these occasions taken her place. "M. Strakosch," he writes, " has gone so far as to sing her part at rehearsals; the initiated have often seen him transformed into ' Rosina,' ' Lucia,' or ' Amina,' replying in character and taking part in a love duet."

Mr. Strakosch, in his "Souvenir d'un Impresario," cites M. de Charnacé's biography of Adelina Patti without saying that in its pages he is misrepresented. The Viennese had, in any case, persuaded themselves that Mr. Strakosch, besides transacting all Adelina Patti's business, sang her parts at rehearsal, and would be prepared even, in case of

need, to render her the same service at the public
performance. A piece was brought out at one of
the minor theatres called *Adelina and her Brother-in-
Law*, in which Strakosch was represented as impersonating her on all possible and impossible occasions.
A visitor called to see Adelina, and was told that
she was not at home, but that Mr. Strakosch would
receive him. A photographer wished to take
Adelina's portrait : " She cannot sit," replies Strakosch, " but I shall be happy to replace her." At
last an infatuated admirer presented himself bent on
making to Adelina a declaration of love : " She is
too much engaged to listen to you," replied the
Strakosch of the farce ; " but anything you may
have to say can be addressed to me."

On July 29th, 1868, Mdlle. Adelina Patti was
married at the Catholic Church of Clapham to the
Marquis de Caux. Among the not very numerous
guests was Signor Mario, who at the breakfast
whispered to me that the Marquis, much as he
might be attached to his fascinating bride, had
never made love to her so much as he, her constant tenor, had done.

The love-making of the tenor from fictitious
becomes at times real, and from the stage passes
into private life. This, some years later, was veri-
fied in the case of Signor Nicolini, Signor Mario's
successor at the Royal Italian Opera, who, apart

from the operatic stage, had become the successor
of the Marquis de Caux. Madame Patti's second
husband was, let it be observed, after the retirement of Mario, the best tenor of his day. His
voice left something to be desired—it was wanting
in firmness ; but he sang with fine dramatic expression, while his acting and general demeanour
recalled at times those of Mario himself. No
one in London has ever sung the tenor part in
Aida as it was sung for some years by Signor
Nicolini. Disapproving of his conduct, however,
the British public also disapproved of his singing;
and at a time when he was still an excellent artist
he disappeared from the stage.

Without malice, and merely as a matter of
operatic history, Maurice Strakosch gives a list of
eminent prime donne whose marriage has been
followed by separation, which in some cases (as in
that of Madame Patti) has again been followed by
a happy union. Among the names he cites are
those of Malibran, Bosio, Frezzolini, Grisi, Lucca,
Trebelli, Marie Sasse and Marie Heilbron. It is the
ambition of every prima donna to get married ; but,
once a wife, she attaches too little importance to
the wedding ring.

It was not until 1878 that Madame Patti visited
Italy. In that year Strakosch engaged her,
together with Signor Nicolini, for a tour which

included the cities of Milan, Genoa, Florence, Rome, and Naples. At Milan the famous prima donna and tenor of the Royal Italian Opera appeared ten times successively in *Aida*. Nowhere had their success been greater than at this celebrated musical city, the capital of Italian Opera; and the triumphs of Milan were repeated in the other Italian cities.

The American tours undertaken by Madame Patti under the auspices and management of Mr. Mapleson carried her to the extremities of civilization and sometimes beyond them.

Madame Patti's life and adventures in the United States as leading lady of Mr. Mapleson's Opera Company have been described in graphic language by scores of American journalists, from whose vivid narratives some extracts may here be given.

"The Mapleson Opera Company," wrote a contributor to the San Francisco *Morning Call*, "did not arrive in a body yesterday. They came one after another, 'like John Brown's cows,' as a disappointed ovation-seeker at the Palace grumblingly said. Patti came about 10 a.m., and went immediately to her rooms, where she requested she might not be disturbed by callers. Other members of the company came before and after. The weather and the uncertainty of arrival prevented the grand reception intended by the Italian colony. However, Patti was met at the Oakland Ferry on her arrival yesterday morning by a committee of Italian citizens under the chairmanship of Mr. Raffe, and accompanied by a band and Prof. D. Speranza's singing school. In the evening she was serenaded at the Palace by the committee of Italian citizens and band and the singing school, which she acknowledged by appearing on the balcony and waving her handkerchief.

" Colonel Mapleson arrived about twelve o'clock. A typical ' John Bull ' of the better class is the gallant Colonel. A tall, broad-shouldered man, whose face shows the blood-lines of health and good living, its roseate hue being heightened by contrast with its frame of richly-silvered hair. Altogether a strong presence has the Colonel, as though the cares of management weigh lightly on him and count as trifles that merely fleck without marring the pleasures of life. A strong voice has he, also—not rough, but mellow as his favourite wine, and suggesting in its deeper notes the possibilities of early training. In response to a *Call*-reporter's query Colonel Mapleson said yesterday : ' I have seen the despatch announcing a probability that Gye will take the Metropolitan Opera-house for next season, but whether true or false the statement does not bother me a whit. It will only be a renewal of our old struggle in London, and this time I have absolutely the whip-hand of him. Of

course if the directors of that institution choose to
put their money on him he will make lively running
for a while, but it will remain to be seen whether he
will ever get as far as the home stretch, to say
nothing of the winning post. I have the great
operatic attractions already secured ; the lesser ones
anyone may have who wants them.

" ' Do I mind being interviewed ? By no means,
if the man who interviews me can write something
that people will read. There is no better form of
advertising, and it generally costs no more than a
little courtesy. Sometimes, of course, one is so
pushed for time that an interview is inconvenient,
but, as a rule, a manager can well afford to talk
with you gentlemen of the fourth estate.'

" ' With your improved mode of travelling,' the
interviewer remarked, ' you must have had a pleasant
trip, Colonel ? '

" ' Oh, delightful and very interesting. Plenty
of room for everybody. The prima donnas had
their different cars. We had three cooks constantly
employed working for ourselves and Patti, and it
was great fun stopping at places and foraging,
capturing chickens and other game. You see we ran
short of provisions, as we were twenty-four hours
overdue. Patti and Gerster are both in excellent
health and fine voice. Patti especially is as lively as a
kitten. Yesterday she seated herself at her piano

in the car, and while breakfast was being prepared sang the celebrated song of the " Queen of Night" from *The Magic Flute*, in the original key, repeatedly striking the highest notes with a bird-like brilliancy, until Nicolini rushed in and, tearing his hair, implored the Diva, if she loved him, not to thus tax her wonderful organ, especially in a railway car.'

" ' It was stated here that you broke up your company in Chicago and sent a great many available people back to New York. Is that so ? '

" ' I have to meet misstatements on every hand. I have to-night here one hundred and eleven people, and that story of my sending fifty-five of my principal chorus singers back is totally untrue. Madame Nordica I had to leave for a certain reason. There were also five of the more aged chorus singers returned, and two had to go home because they shortly expected to become mothers.

" ' Our success along the road,' said the Colonel with a still brighter manner, ' has been wonderful. It surpassed everything I expected, Denver in particular. Why, at Cheyenne the Legislature and Assembly adjourned, and they chartered a special car to meet us sixty miles out. It was a fine compliment. The car was piled full of champagne and cigars, some of the finest I ever smoked. This is a great country, surely! On arriving at Cheyenne

the band of the Ninth Regiment, in full dress parade
uniform, was in attendance, and the whole population turned out, barring a few sick children and old
people, who were obliged to be left at home.   The
total population of Cheyenne by the last census is
only 4,000 people, and there were 3,000 at the
opera that night at 10 dols. a ticket.   What do you
think of that ?   We were afterwards entertained by
the Mayor at the Club, which is one of the best-
appointed I have seen in the United States, and we
left amid cheering and music by the band.'

" ' How many performances do you propose to give
in this city, Colonel ? '

" ' The number depends on circumstances and the
support extended by the public.   So long as you
people want us we will try to do our best.   I am at
present negotiating to get rid of singing in Cincinnati, and, if successful, shall be enabled to give three
more nights here.'

" ' There was a great feeling of disappointment
among us at first when it was given out that Madame
Patti did not intend to come.'

" ' I can well understand that.   Patti at first
resolved not to visit California professionally, only
to get a glimpse of the country and the natural
curiosities about which we had all heard so much.
People told her about San Francisco until she
longed to see the city, and finding her in a fitting

mood I persuaded her to sing, and have made arrangements to that effect. While she was crossing the bay this morning she seemed to drink in its grandeur and that of the surrounding scenery with delight, and when we landed the broad, clean streets and fresh look of the buildings filled her with enthusiasm. " What a heavenly place," she cried ; " I would like to sing here to-night." I told her I would take prompt steps to meet her wishes, but she must restrain herself for the present.'

" ' And she will sing ? '

" ' Certainly ; but not before Thursday evening, and it will tax all my energies to carry out her wishes even then. She will appear in her great character of " Violetta " in *La Traviata*. I propose to give also one Patti concert, the date of which will be hereafter announced.

" ' One difficulty, as at first supposed,' continued the Colonel, ' in regard to Patti's appearance, was that she had not got her new dresses here yet. She left most of her trunks at Chicago. They had just arrived there, and as she was told the railroad people charge heavily for extra baggage she did not bring them. But they have been telegraphed for, and they will be here in time. Those dresses are of the most costly description. They were made by Madame Morin, of Paris, the rival of Worth. Patti had to get permission of the syndicate of dress-

makers, formed in Paris to establish the season's
fashions, to wear these dresses in advance of their
fiat, and the ladies of San Francisco will thus have
the privilege of studying what the fair dames of
London, Paris, and New York are doing, and be
enabled to lead the fashions.'

" ' What will be the extra charge to hear Madame
Patti ?'

" ' The prices will be announced to-morrow. I
am anxious to please the public, who have placed
such confidence in me and who have subscribed so
liberally. As Patti's engagement was only made
after the official programme was issued I have
arranged that season ticket-holders will have priority
of selection for the Patti performance at a reduction
of twenty per cent. from the ordinary ticket-buyer.'

" ' Opera is a great luxury, Colonel, if the prices
paid the singer are as high as stated.'

" ' I believe you, my boy. Cast your eyes over
these vouchers, and you'll be satisfied.' Here he
showed some formidable figures, cheques, and receipts. 'Patti gets 5,000 dols. a night; she
only gets half that in London. Gerster and all
the rest in the same proportion. Yet we charge
more for admission in London than in the United
States. The London prices are from 10 dols. to
100 dols. for private boxes on Patti nights. The
price of the stalls is one guinea (5 dols. 25 c.);

pit, 10s. 6d. (2 dols. 62½ c.) ; gallery, 5s. (1 dol.
25 c.). These are theatre prices. It is quite
common for the principal and best seats to be bought
up by leading music-dealers, who advance the price
in accordance with the occasion—sometimes from
three to ten guineas. Excepting Patti all my people
get salary while crossing the Continent—a nice little
bill, to say nothing of 20,000 dols. I have to pay
for the special train there and back.

" ' By the way,' continued the Colonel, ' you
ought to go and see those cars—Patti's car especially.
It is one of the most elegant affairs imaginable ; the
best, I think, that was ever contrived by the ingenuity of man. The walls are covered with embossed
leather, the painting by Parisian artists ; it is in
cloth of gold, and cost 65,000 dols. There are also
three other boudoir cars, including " La Traviata,"
occupied by Galassi, Arditi, Carraccioli, and Lom-
bardelli ; and " La Sonnambula," occupied by other
principal artists. I occupied the " Lycoming," where
I entertained Madame Gerster, Madame Dotti, and
Count Zacharoff. Have you met Zacharoff, let me
ask ? '

" ' Not yet.'

" ' Ah ! He's a rather remarkable man. Fought
all through the Russian war, and is rich now, I
believe. Owns black diamonds, and all that sort of
thing.'

" ' It is generally hoped, Colonel,' the interviewer remarked, 'that this visit to our city will not be your last; that Francisco will be included in your operatic circuit for the future.'

" ' Ah ! my dear fellow, my heart says " Yes " to that hope; but I do not know what my pocket is going to say on the subject, although from appearances I think my purse will say " Yes " to it. I never, at a first glance, was so struck with a place as I am with this city. In the early part of May I return to London. The new Opera-house which is being built for me there will not be ready till May, 1885, when it will be opened by Madame Adelina Patti. It is being built on the Thames Embankment, next to the House of Parliament, larger than La Scala, and it will be called the National Opera-house. Between my arrival and the opening of the National I shall get my first rest in twenty-four years, and I intend touring Europe to recruit my company for next season. I have heard of some wonderful voices in different parts of the world.'

" ' Where ? '

" ' Where ? Well, my dear boy ' (with a droop of the eyelid and a slightly cunning expression of face), ' I do not think I will mention that even to you just yet. Patti, when she concludes her American season, will go to her castle in Wales, where she will stay till the latter part of June, entertaining in her usual lavish manner. I believe the Prince and Princess of Wales are likely to pay her the oft-promised visit this year. [This visit has not yet come off.] When she returns to London she will sing five or six times at Covent Garden.'

" ' I presume, Colonel, that you are always on the look-out for exceptional voices.'

" ' Good singers are as scarce as satisfied prima donnas. I am constantly on the alert for lyric talent, such as the public will accept, but it is quite a lottery. For each singer who has made any mark on the stage there are ninety-nine failures. You'll get many a blank, I can tell you, before you draw a prize. It is an expensive operation. At the present time there are nearly 2,000 Americans studying in Italy and various parts of Germany, all more or less showing great aptitude, and I always give preference to Americans. Why, look at the list of Americans I have been the means of placing on the operatic stage in England. Patti is an American to all intents and purposes, as she was reared in the United States. In 1860 I took her to England and brought her out ; in 1862 I presented Clara Louise Kellog to the London public ; in 1868 Minnie Hauk ; in 1869 Annie Louise Carey ; in 1870 Miss Valleria, of Baltimore ; in 1871 Florence Rix, Knox, and Jules Perkins, the basso ; in 1874, Cardidus the tenor, and also Henry Stanfield ; in 1875 Maria Litta ; in 1876 Emma Abbott ;

in 1877 Marie Van Zandt, whom I had placed under tuition for five years previously; in 1879 Emma Nevada; in 1880 Dotti, now in my company, and in 1883 Nordica. I am now negotiating with Jennie Sergeant, Louise Lester, who is known here, and others of whom great things are expected.'

" ' Colonel, your attitude towards Mr. Abbey has been a subject of much newspaper comment. What is your opinion of Henry ? '

" ' I look upon Abbey as a very able theatrical speculator—a speculator in the fullest sense of the term, as he will take up anything from which money can be extracted. Why he entered the Italian Opera field to ruin himself I cannot for a moment imagine. I predicted his downfall at the very outset, which you might have seen by some early interviews I had in New York with the *Herald* and *Evening Post* a year ago, when I named within 1,000 dols. the very sum he would lose. His losses, as set forth in the schedule which has been prepared, are over 260,000 dols., and that in a space of two months and a half. He simply entered the operatic field to wipe me out, as it were. He and his seven brother shareholders have a little pool of their own, and are interested in bringing out anything they imagine there is money in and will send them off well. There is the case of Sarah Bernhardt, who is thought nothing of on the other side, then Langtry, and now Irving. They estimated it would cost 100,000 dols. to remove me, and they raised it, but it was no go. I am still to the front, ready to meet the next comer. Abbey knows nothing, and when he finishes his ten nights in New York commencing to-morrow he quits the operatic arena for good.'

"(And here the Colonel rose and bunched some telegrams as a hint that other matters were pressing.) 'I have got a lease of the Academy of Music in New York for seven years, which I can get extended, and I may say again that I am so pleased with my first impressions of California that if I can only meet my expenses I shall be more than repaid for my visit.'

"'Entrez,' responded a pleasant voice to his tap on the door, as the *Call* reporter stepped from a dark corridor of the Palace Hotel into one of the most charming apartments in that gigantic caravansary. The air that greeted his incoming was so warm and so laden with the perfume of flowers that for an instant he thought himself in a conservatory rather than a drawing-room, and glanced around for the exotics that must be harboured in this cosy nook. At first his eye lighted on a pyramid of bouquets, built up on the table, then upon more bouquets on chairs, sofas, and even strewn over the floor for lack of other resting place. Then his attention was caught by a beautiful parrot fluttering against the bars of its cage; next by a silver-haired gentleman

rising slowly from his seat; and finally by a charming little lady, who said in a tone of assumed pique:
' Will you deign to turn your eyes in this direction,
monsieur ? I'm a little body, to be sure, but then I
am really seeable if one only tries to see me out.'
The one rare exotic of this hothouse had been found,
and the wandering eyes of the reporter from that
moment ceased their wandering. A winsome lady
is Madame Patti, in face, in figure, in speech, and in
ways of gesture; in fact, she is precisely described
by that intranslatable French expression, *très chic.*
The passing years have tripped so lightly by this
favourite of fortune that she seems to mock the
record of her birth, and to be almost as young as
when she sang with Mario, twenty years ago. Sparkling eyes, piquante and mobile features, nervous, bird-
like gestures, clear but rapid utterance, a small, compactly built figure, a profusion of dark, wavy hair,
a costume becoming in the extreme—and behold
Madame Adelina Patti, as she appeared yesterday
afternoon. After a few complimentary nothings
had been said the Diva laughingly remarked : ' According to every physical rule I should be a very
tired little woman to-day, but *au contraire* I am so
filled with the electricity of novelty and excitement
that I really haven't time to grow weary. Everything possible has been arranged for my comfort in
travelling, but the weather has been so very naughty

that it gave me no rest at all last night. Then these
wash-ups—wash-ins—wash-outs—how is it you call
them?—have made such long delays that it really
seemed as though we should never reach this Mecca
of our hopes. Just think of it, we were stopped ten,
seven, some tremendous number of hours at one of
these washing places alone. Now that we have got
here it is raining—but that won't last long—do say
it won't! If you only knew how much I have wanted
to see the bright sunny California that travellers tell
about, you would say a prayer on my behalf to the
Clerk of the Weather. California has been so long
the dream of my anticipation, and yet, do you know,
I came very near not getting here at all. I don't
think I could have resisted the temptation to come,
however, even if the present engagement had not
been made, for I had several spare weeks on my
hands and could not have employed them better
than to make the trip for pleasure simply. I shall
probably never visit America again—as a singer, that
is—and it would have been shameful to have missed
the hospitable reception that artists are accorded on
this coast. At least, so they all tell me, those who
have been here. Ah! if you but knew how much
has been done to prevent my coming; but I have
come, and am consequently in humour to smile on
everybody and everything.'

"'Do you absolutely mean, madame,' inquired the

reporter, 'that you shall never return to America in a professional capacity — that the present season will be your last one in this country ?'

" *Mais non*; I will not say it *absolument*, for I may possibly return once more for a farewell engagement. That is in the dim distance, however; and, understand, that a farewell engagement with me means exactly what it says. I have no wish to continue on the stage after my voice has gone, as so many, many other artists have done, but want to close my operatic career before my friends will need to apologize for my vocal failings. That is why I was so glad to come to America this year—for really without an extra amount of vanity, I can say that I never sang better than at present; and it is so delightful to feel that you will not disappoint the good, kind, lovely public by giving them a faded imitation of your former self.'

" At this point several other visitors entered the room and the interview merged into general chat. Among the new-comers was a Russian gentleman, at present residing in this city, and when the ex-interviewer called Madame Patti's attention to this fact she beamed upon that Russian, and took him, metaphorically speaking, to her heart. ' Ah,' said she, ' how I dote on Russia! So many of my happiest hours have been passed there. Such audiences were never seen as those of St. Petersburg. Do not

understand me to be ungrateful for the kindness
shown me in so many other countries'—this aside
to her American guests—'but those brave Russians
are so enthusiastic over what they like. It is worth
ten years of one's life to be a favourite for one night
in St. Petersburg. They avalanche their applause
upon you after a successful effort until you feel as
happy as an angel. I have been called out again
and again until I had no strength to stand any
longer, and then was obliged to sit on a chair
upon the stage and wait until the audience would
let me go.

"'You saw me there? Then I must shake hands
with you again, for your heart must have shared in
my triumph. Do you remember how the dear old
Empress used to make tea for me between the acts?
God bless her! and that grand old gentleman, the
Czar, who used to let me call him "papa!" Ah,
me! How I shall miss them both. They were so
dignified, and yet so gentle with little me. I shall
always love Russia and the Russians for their sakes.
I am to be in St. Petersburg next season—St.
Petersburg! why, my blood already starts at the
thought of the welcome old friends will give me.'

"The door again opened, this time without a
warning tap, and a pleasant looking gentleman
entered, and after standing a moment said, in quite
passable English and with a smile, 'Is it necessary
that I introduce myself?'

" ' Messieurs,' replied Madame Patti, also smiling brightly, ' allow me to present to your kindly acquaintance Signor Nicolini. Ah, *mon ami !* ' to him, ' you see here the Press and Russia; to both I owe so many favours that you will be glad to meet their representatives.'

"'The interview was now further off than ever, for the conversation turned to all sorts of uninterviewable, but, for all that, pleasant subjects, the main point being a discussion of Colonel Mapleson's business chances in San Francisco. As a last effort to catch the lost thread of his intended interview, the reporter finally asked Madame Patti to name some of the operas in which she prefers to appear.

" ' I could name many that I like, but if you mean the few I most love—*Lucia, Sonnambula, Traviata, Il Barbiere,* and *Romeo and Juliet*—the last especially, for it requires two first-class artists to sing it, and those two carry the entire opera. It is difficult, and so generally a failure, that one must feel proud to make a success of it.'

" As the interviewer rose to take his leave his charming hostess said —

" ' If you write anything about me, be sure you say something nice, for if you do not, I'll—I'll not spend five cents to buy your paper.'

" Then she laughed merrily and continued —

" ' Do one thing for me, please ; say that my heart feels very warmly towards the new friends who have

welcomed me so kindly to your city by the sea.
Look round you at all these flowers, and tell me if
I have not reason to be grateful. That pyramid of
bouquets came from a party of young girls, whose
faces were brighter than the flowers they brought,
and I shall treasure them as memories of a pleasant
meeting. Please say so for me, for I mean it.' ''*

To attempt any complete appreciation of Madame
Patti in the various parts she has undertaken would
be out of the question, so numerous have they been.
Her admirers, however, have missed something if
by chance any of them have not seen her in perhaps
the most characteristic of all her impersonations :
that of " Rosina," in which (to borrow a happy
expression from the Russian critic, the late Lenz)
she shows herself, at each fresh appearance, "*plus
Patti que jamais.*"   " Rosina " is a part which
the composer may be said to have treated on
what, in the language of commerce, is called the
" double entry system."   It secures two first appearances for the prima donna ; and though this very
arrangement is said to have been one of the
causes of the disfavour with which the masterpiece
was received on its first production (when it was
hissed by many and applauded by no one except
the half-ironical, half-indignant composer, who
stood up manfully for what he knew to be an

achievement of some merit), it renders *Il Barbiere* a
very suitable opera in which to reintroduce a
thoroughly popular artist. "Rosina" appears first
of all in the balcony, where she is received with the
applause of recognition. This is renewed when she
comes on in the second scene, which might well be
considered a second act, to sing the long-delayed
air out of which the Roman audience of the year
1815 fancied the original "Rosina" meant to
defraud them. There is yet another opportunity
for touching the heart of the public—ready, in the
case of Madame Patti, to respond with the greatest
warmth to the very slightest advances—when "Dr.
Bartolo's" interesting ward takes her music-lesson;
and the culminating point is reached when the fall
of the curtain cannot but be accepted as a sign for
recalling the heroine of the evening, and offering
her the homage which she has earned anew by one
more fascinating performance.

The comic and the serious author in *Le Diable
Boiteux*, after exchanging fulsome compliments,
disputed as to which of their respective styles was
most difficult, and thereupon came to blows.
Madame Adelina Patti, if any such question as
this were to arise in connection with operatic performances, might take either side at will. Those
who may have seen her only in great dramatic parts
will not be likely to admit that comedy is her *forte*.

Those who are, above all, familiar with her
" Rosina " in *Il Barbiere,* or her " Norina " in
Don Pasquale, may well believe that she was
born to represent the heroines of lyrical comedy.
But the fact is her dramatic genius has as extended
a range as her own beautiful voice, every accent of
humour, of sentiment, and of passion being equally
at her command.   Without, however, attempting to
decide which of the two styles is the most difficult,
it may safely be said that the comic style—or, to be
precise, the style of comedy—is the most rare.

We have several " Aminas," many " Marthas,"
a remarkably large number of " Margheritas ; " but
we have only one " Rosina," and Madame Patti,
rising constantly to new heights, and embellishing
the music year after year with ornamentation of a
more dazzling description, would seem to take a
malicious pleasure in placing the part farther and
farther beyond the reach of all other vocalists.

If any other artist were able to sing Rossini's
brilliant music more or less as Madame Patti sings
it, the difficulty of impersonating the character as
we are accustomed to see it impersonated by the
perfect " Rosina " of the Royal Italian Opera would
still remain.   *Qui dit Rosina, pense Patti* has been
well said by the author of " Beethoven et ses trois
styles," who, after a long course of symphonies and
sonatas, seems to have found true musical happiness

in listening to Italian music as sung by the greatest operatic artist of our time; and the manner in which Madame Patti identifies herself with the character he names is indeed perfect.

When such singing as comes from the mouth of " Rosina " is heard, the most convinced Wagnerian must be led to reflect that if the Wagnerian system were established on the operatic stage to the exclusion of all others there would be no place for such vocalization as may be heard from the lips of Madame Patti. If Wagner had not aimed at universal dominion he might not have gained even so much space as has been accorded to him at the great Opera-houses of Europe. But it is well to remember that the adoption of the Wagnerian system, to the neglect of every other, involves the absolute—too absolute—subjection of the vocalist. The prima donna, flightiest of the whole flock of human singing-birds, would be caught, clipped, and imprisoned within the iron cage of dramatic necessity.

Without denying the poetic beauty of *Tannhäuser* and *Lohengrin*, it is impossible not to see that the abandonment of the lyrical stage to such works would involve the sacrifice of singing as an art; of singing for the sake of singing such as the public applauds with enthusiasm whenever it has an opportunity of hearing Madame Patti in a thoroughly vocal part. Madame Patti can equally awaken the admiration of her audience when she undertakes characters in which a strict adherence to the musical text is required. But of the various kinds of excellence which together make up her incomparable talent, one is perfection as a vocalist; and it is only in genuine Italian Opera, and chiefly in the works of Rossini, that this excellence can be displayed.

Another favourite part of Madame Patti's, one of those in which she loved to appear at the beginning of each new season, was that of " Catarina" in Meyerbeer's *Etoile du Nord.* In the original *Etoile du Nord* we find the so-called " opéra comique" in its fullest possible development. It would be grand opera, if it could. It presents the most astounding and literally stunning combinations of vocal and instrumental masses that were ever heard on the stage. Indeed, *L'Etoile du Nord* would scarcely be intelligible as an " opéra comique" but for the known fact that before being presented in that conventional shape it had a prior existence as a " grand opera" of the German pattern. Its principal pieces were composed for the *Camp of Silesia,* from which they were detached to serve, amid entirely new surroundings, in the opera to which they at present belong. The principal part in the *Camp of Silesia* was written for Jenny Lind, who is

known to have sung with great success the air with
double flute accompaniment, now forming the chief
musical feature of the third act of *L'Etoile du Nord.*
Frederick the Great, flute-player and warrior, was
the leading character in the *Camp of Silesia;* and
one can see the traces of his warlike and flute-play-
ing tendencies even in the imitation work, of which
not " Frederick II.," but " Peter I.," is the hero.
The real value in music of what is called " local
colour" is sufficiently shown by the fact that what
was considered appropriate colour for a Prussian subject is considered equally appropriate for a Russian.
The march which now does duty in *L'Etoile du
Nord* as a Russian march is, as a matter of fact,
one of the historical marches of the Prussian Army.
The choruses of Finnish peasants in the dockyard
scene of the first act are quaint; and being outlandish in character pass for Finnish, as they might
equally, according to circumstances, pass for Persian
or Babylonian. The so-called " gipsy-rondo," sung
by " Catarina," is original and melodious ; but it
would be difficult to say what gipsy feature it
possesses. Nor is it at all clear why " Catherine,"
the future wife of " Peter," should be presented as
a gipsy.

Apart from history, "Catarina" is one of the great
comic opera family to which the " Catarina " of *Les
Diamants de la Couronne,* " Angèle " of *Le Domino*

Noir, and so many more of Scribe's heroines belong.
In each successive act she appears not only in a new
costume, but also in a new character. Indeed, the
third act exhibits her in two characters, and the first
in two, if not three. In Act I. we see " Catarina,"
first, as the daughter of a Finnish innkeeper;
secondly, as a gipsy; thirdly, as an enterprising
young girl starting on her travels in man's clothes.
In Act II. she is a soldier, in a tunic and cocked
hat. In Act III. she is, in the first scene, the conventional operatic lunatic, arrayed in pure white, with
her hair hanging loose on her shoulders; and in the
last the Empress of all the Russias, clad in Imperial
purple, and crowned with the Imperial diadem.
L'Etoile du Nord is the most varied, and by far the
most incoherent, of all Meyerbeer's works. Made
up out of the remains of an earlier opera, it doubtless
owes its patchiness to that fact. Scribe, most
accommodating, as he was also the most ingenious,
of librettists, must have been asked to furnish a
" book " which would enable the composer to bring
in some of the characters, some of the situations,
and all the principal musical pieces of the *Camp of
Silesia.* Throwing history, ethnology, probability,
nature, and art to the winds, Scribe produced *L'Etoile
du Nord;* than which a stranger, more inconsistent,
more indigestible mixture of fact and fiction was
never presented on any stage.

Add to this that the principal man's part is gloomy and for the bass voice, that the hero distinguishes himself in one long scene which occupies nearly the whole of the second act by getting heroically and tragically drunk, and that the finale to this same act introduces a chorus and two military bands on the stage which, playing different themes, are heard in combination with the full orchestra playing yet another theme, and no further inquiry need be made as to why *L'Etoile du Nord* is, of all Meyerbeer's operas, the heaviest.

So strikingly dull was the third act after Meyerbeer had, with a view to the Royal Italian Opera, put M. Scribe's dialogue into recitative, that it was found absolutely necessary to relieve it by means of a new and, in a dramatic point of view, most unnecessary air for the tenor, the result being that " Peter," " Danilowitz," and " Catarina " have now, one after the other, to sing a solo in two verses. Thus the opening scenes of the third act form a sort of "ballad concert," which "Catarina's" solo (No. 3 of the series) at last brings to an end.

The Prussian *Camp of Silesia* was a much simpler work than the quasi-Russian *Etoile du Nord;* for which Scribe substituted a new libretto to do duty in connection with old music—a new canvas beneath old colours. In Rellstab's not very dramatic

piece, Frederick runs the risk of being captured
by "Pandours" during the Silesian campaign; and
it was to match this incident that Scribe made "Cal-
mucks" threaten the safety of Peter in Finland!
The attention of the Hungarians is occupied and
their rage calmed by the gipsy, "Vielka," who sings
to them the spirited and charming rondo which
"Catarina" (a gipsy for ten minutes) was afterwards to sing to the Tartars who had so strangely
found their way to Finland. All the military music
which plays so important a part in the second act of
L'Etoile du Nord belonged originally to the *Camp
of Silesia.* So, among other pieces, did the air,
with accompaniment of two flutes, which Madame
Patti sings so perfectly in the third act of *L'Etoile
du Nord* and in which Jenny Lind used to achieve
a brilliant success.

Madame Adelina Patti has generally made her
first reappearance for the season either as "Violetta"
or as "Rosina;" and every opera-goer knows that
as the heroine of Beaumarchais and Rossini's admirable musical comedy she is incomparable. There
are other parts, however, in which she is almost
equally admirable, and in which she is equally content to make, as the French say, her *rentrée*. One
of these is the part of "Catarina" in Meyerbeer's
Etoile du Nord. There is certainly none which
offers more variety at once of costume and of style;

and the question of costume is taken into consideration even by so great an artist as Madame Patti.
"Rosina" is always the same ; and so charming is
she as impersonated by Madame Patti that no one
can reasonably complain of her never for one
moment losing her identity. Change, however, is
often agreeable in itself ; and those who wish to see
and hear Madame Patti in as many costumes and as
many characters as possible cannot do better than
witness the performance of *L'Etoile du Nord*, with
Madame Patti assuming turn by turn in that work
the part of a waiting-maid at an inn, of a fortune-tell-
ing gipsy, a young recruit, a sentinel, a young lady
clothed in melancholy and white muslin, and finally
a princess sound in body as in mind and decked in
robes of splendour.   In *L'Etoile du Nord* we see on
the stage not one Patti, but six Pattis.

The French *Etoile du Nord*, in spite of its vast
proportions, was not composed or rearranged for the
stage of a large theatre. It reappeared in its second
incarnation at the Opéra Comique of Paris, where
the part of " Catarina " was charmingly sung by
Mdlle. Caroline Duprez. But the theatre was
not large enough for the work. The combined
finale of Act II. had an absolutely stunning effect ;
and the most successful piece in the opera was the
duel and duet in the tent scene for the two lively
and pugnacious *vivandières*. At the Opéra Comique

the three masses of voices and instruments which are introduced in the finale to the second act, first in succession, then in combination, were of necessity brought too closely together. At the Royal Italian Opera the different bodies of troops with their different orchestras and different melodies have space to move in; and the themes played by the three orchestras can be made out with something like distinctness.

But, in spite of its ingenuity, the concerted finale to the second act of *L'Etoile du Nord* is more aston-ishing than agreeable.

It may seem ungrateful to examine too closely a work which, with all its inconsistencies and defects, contains a great deal of beautiful music and a part which is charming even among the many charming parts included in Madame Patti's rich and varied repertory. More brilliant singing than that of Madame Patti in the scene of the last act has never been heard. Nor could anything, in its way, be more admirable than her delivery of the couplets in narrative of the first act. The prayer, too, at the end of this act—the most beautiful melody in the opera—is always sung by her with the deepest and purest expression, as the sparkling barcarolle which follows it is thrown off with the most exquisite lightness.

When *L'Etoile du Nord* was first presented at the

Royal Italian Opera, the recitatives furnished by
Meyerbeer in lieu of the spoken dialogue of the French
original made the work tedious. The first act went
brilliantly enough, but the second, in which a great
dramatic situation had to be written up to, was full
of preparatory and explanatory talk, such as in
opera should as much as possible be dispensed with.
And in the third act so much recitative is presented that Meyerbeer himself seems to have taken
fright and in his alarm to have felt the necessity of introducing a suitable air for the tenor;
an air in which the accompaniment of ascending
scales for two flutes is more remarkable than the
rather common-place theme. But even in the days
of its first production on the stage of the Royal
Italian Opera, those who remained to see the
end of this very tiring third act were well rewarded by the beautiful scena for the prima donna.
They are doubly rewarded when the prima donna is
Adelina Patti.

No one can have an idea of the full range of
Madame Patti's histrionic genius who, in addition to
the parts of " Rosina " and "Catarina," has not also
seen her in that of "Dinorah." There are plenty of
fantastic characters in opera; but of characters at
once fantastic, graceful, and consistent there is not
one that can be placed on a level with that of the
heroine in *Le Pardon de Ploermel.* " Dinorah " re-

calls in some measure *La Petite Fadette* of George
Sand. But she has, thanks to Meyerbeer, her own
musical physiognomy, and, thanks to Madame Patti,
her own musical expression. Written for one of the
most brilliant vocalists of the period, the part
abounds in difficulties which, as treated by Madame
Patti, are only so many opportunities for the display
of consummate facility. "Dinorah," as a singer, is
passing over the loftiest and slenderest bridges, and
by the side of the most dangerous precipices, not in
the scene of the cataract alone, but throughout the
opera. Apart from dazzling flights in the highest
region of the vocal register, "Dinorah" has passages
of simple expression which are not, perhaps, more
truly melodious than those with which they form so
striking a contrast, but which are melodious in another
manner. What, for instance, can be more beautiful
than the lullaby of the first act—as full of tenderness
as a song of Schubert's? "Lullaby to an intract-
able goat," it might be called; for the ungrateful
creature refuses only too often to be caressed by the
voice of the charmer, even if it does not (as sometimes happens) turn the solo into a duet by introducing unmusical notes of its own. Meyerbeer was
fond of animals; and had he carried out the intention
he seems at one time to have entertained of setting
Faust to music, he would doubtless have added to
the horse of *Les Huguenots* and the goat of

"Dinorah" the dog which so naturally becomes transformed into cynical Mephistopheles.

Gounod's *Roméo et Juliette,* in which the composer is always pleasing, though seldom impressive, might be described as the powerful drama of *Romeo and Juliet* reduced to the proportions of an eclogue for "Juliet" and " Romeo." One remembers the work as a series of very pretty duets, varied by a sparkling waltz air for " Juliet," and one really dramatic scene, also for " Juliet," in which Madame Patti displays that tragic genius which belongs to her equally with the highest capacity for comedy. *Romeo e Giulietta* is an admirable opera for " Giulietta ;" in which " Romeo " is not forgotten.

Madame Patti's first appearance for the season in *La Traviata* never fails to fill the house ; and by the time " Violetta " has primed herself with champagne and advanced to the footlights, glass in hand, to sing " Libiamo " there is never a vacant place in the theatre. The story of *La Dame aux Camélias* has been so purified in its conversion from its original dramatic form into the libretto of an opera that " Violetta's " stage business with the champagne in the opening scene is really all that remains to stamp her as a " transgressor " of a particular kind ; and, without fastidiousness, it might be wished that " Violetta " would not throw her champagne about the stage, which, besides being a little unbecoming, would in actual life be imprudent, as some of it might fall on her dress.   It belongs to the part, however, and has to be done; and such being the case who could do it more gracefully than Madame Patti?   After that only too characteristic drinking song, "Violetta," as everyone knows, bids farewell to her life of reckless gaiety, and only resumes it in a moment of despair, when she feels that she must shortly bid farewell to life altogether. The part is full of the most dramatic contrasts; and in that, as in the real merit of the alternately brilliant and pathetic music, is to be found the simple explanation of the favour with which it is regarded by prime donne and by the public.   In Madame Patti's "Violetta" there is always something new to be observed; new ornamentation in the cadences of the principal airs, new points of inspiration in the acting, and new dresses of the most tasteful kind in every scene.

"Semiramide" is one of Madame Patti's latest impersonations; and the announcement that she would appear in a part usually undertaken by vocalists of a different type caused in the first instance some surprise.   Mr. Gye had been looking abroad year after year for a tolerable "Semiramide," when he had an incomparable one in his own company.   This was to be explained by the widespread, though not very ancient, delusion as to the existence of two distinct classes of soprano singers—the light and the heavy—otherwise the "dramatic." The late Madame Grisi and the late Mademoiselle Titiens distinguished themselves in "dramatic" parts, among which "Norma," "Lucrezia Borgia," and "Semiramide" were all included. As "Semiramide," both Madame Grisi and Mademoiselle Titiens obtained great success, and both were "robust," not only of voice, but also of person. Hence the notion that "Semiramide" must necessarily be represented by a singer possessing a voice of large calibre, with figure to match.

Yet Mademoiselle Titiens was slim enough when she first undertook in this country the part of "Semiramide;" and it was not because she was tall, but because she was a great artist, that she made so much impression in that character. It was considered, all the same, a matter of course that though Madame Patti might represent to perfection such personages as "Amina," "Lucia," "Linda," "Gilda," "Rosina," "Dinorah," and some dozen others, more or less of the same type, yet the repertory of the so-called dramatic *soprano* must remain closed to her. Accordingly, since the retirement of Madame Grisi, Mr. Gye had sent to the uttermost ends of the operatic earth in search of "dramatic *soprani*." Some of the would-be "Semiramides" possessed the supposed physical

requirements of the part almost in excess; but not
one of them could get herself accepted by the public
as a fair representative of the Assyrian queen.   As
a matter of fact, there is no reason for supposing
that "Semiramide" was more "robust" than
"Cleopatra;" and no one can suppose the fascinating "serpent of the Nile" to have been otherwise
than lithe and supple in figure.   It was not, however, until after several "Semiramides" of a larger
growth had proved themselves incapable of grap-
pling with the music and with the meaning of the
part that the manager of the Royal Italian Opera
thought of the artist who had shown herself, in
Ernani, Aida, &c., a great tragic actress, and who
had been known long before—ever since her first
season in England—to be an accomplished mistress
of such vocalization as the florid music of Rossini
demands.   It might, moreover, have been remembered that the part of "Semiramide" had been
sung with brilliant success by Madame Sontag and
by Madame Bosio, who thirty years ago appeared
as "Semiramide" at Paris and at St. Petersburg.

Indeed, the very music would seem to show that,
far from being unsuited to the light soprano voice,
the part could only receive justice at the hands of a
singer possessing the peculiar gifts and acquirements
by which the light soprano is distinguished.   Rossini,
who probably knew how his own music should be

sung, was delighted when he heard that Adelina Patti wished some day to appear as " Semiramide ; " and to give additional brilliancy to her performance he wrote for her the ornaments which she now introduces in " Semiramide's " great *aria*, " Bel raggio." He at the same time wrote, in view of their being sung by Madame Patti, new passages for " Desdemona's " willow song.

That Madame Patti would find all the music of *Semiramide* well within her resources must have been known beforehand to all who had ever heard her in a Rossinian opera. Others who had heard her repeatedly in every part she had undertaken were, moreover, aware that her impersonation would, in a dramatic point of view, be all that could be desired. Madame Patti does not walk the stage like a conventional stage queen, with measured step, lofty bearing, and head slightly thrown back in token of general disdain. Always natural, always entering into the spirit of the character she impersonates, she is queenly, not through any deliberate assumption of royal airs (which are as easily put on as scarlet robes), but because in the exercise of her high dramatic faculty she becomes " Semiramide " herself. She is as queenly as it is possible to be without ceasing to be womanly.

Madame Patti may now be said, so far as Europe is concerned, to have quitted the operatic stage.

So extravagant are her terms that no manager can engage her for performances in which it is necessary that she should be supported by singers of something like her own artistic value. She has taken farewell of art as she practised it in her early days; and she has for some time past been engaged in making, by means of her immense reputation and her undiminished talent, a colossal fortune. Such, however, has been the history of most previous " stars," dramatic as well as operatic; and if Madame Patti is now profiting by her fame, it must be remembered that this fame was originally due to genuine artistic success gained successively in every European capital.

Madame Patti has never sung in one of Wagner's operas; differing in this respect from Madame Lucca, Madame Nilsson, Mademoiselle de Murska, and Madame Albani.

CHAPTER V.

MADAME PAULINE LUCCA belongs to the same period
as Madame Adelina Patti and Madame Christine
Nilsson, and was born in the same year. She first
attracted attention in 1856, when, as a young girl,
she was singing in the choir of the Karlskirche at
Vienna. Here her beautiful voice was much remarked; and the Karlskirche was attended by many
persons who might have reproached themselves, like
St. Augustine, with paying more attention to the
singing than to what was being sung. About a
century before Sophie Arnould had in like manner
drawn numbers of persons to the convent chapel,
where on Sundays and holidays she habitually
sang.

Soon afterwards Pauline Lucca joined the Vienna
Opera-house, accepting in the first instance an

engagement in the chorus; but chorus-master, musical director, and manager soon saw that in the sweet-voiced, bright-mannered Pauline they had no ordinary chorus-girl to deal with. She was entrusted with the solo verses of the "Bridesmaids' chorus" in *Der Freishütz*, and sang them so charmingly that people crowded to the Opera-house for the express purpose of hearing them. The young vocalist had already accepted an engagement for Olmütz, where she was to sing principal parts, or she would at once have begun at Vienna her career as prima donna.

At Olmütz in 1859, two years before Adelina Patti came out in London, Pauline Lucca appeared as "Elvira" in *Ernani*. From Olmütz she went to Prague, where, in 1860, she caused the greatest enthusiasm by her impersonation of "Valentine" in *Les Huguenots*. Meyerbeer had now heard of her, and when, in 1861, she came to Berlin, he recognized in her his ideal "Selika." He had long been seeking a fit representative for the heroine in what was to prove his last opera; and probably had Pauline Lucca been able to sing in French he would have recommended her for the part to the management of the French Opera-house. Here the character a few years afterwards was to be created by a more experienced, but less youthful, vocalist, Madame Sax—or Sasse, as she was ordered to call herself in the bills, when it was proved before a tribunal that she had abandoned her rightful name to usurp the one borne by the estimable inventor of a whole family of keyed wind-instruments.

In 1863 Madame Pauline Lucca made her first appearance at the Royal Italian Opera, where Patti, since 1861, had been the reigning star. Here her most successful impersonations were " Margherita " in *Faust* (which for many seasons she played alternately with Madame Patti) ; " Valentine " in *Les Huguenots,* a part for which she was scarcely fitted by her not very imposing figure, but which she sang with fine dramatic feeling; " Zerlina " in *Fra Diavolo;* and, above all, perhaps, " Cherubino " in the *Marriage of Figaro.* In the part of " Cherubino," Lucca was so charming and so much like the Chérubin of Beaumarchais himself (a little toned down in Mozart's thoroughly beautiful setting) that a very illustrious singer is said to have objected to take the part of " Susanna " in a singularly perfect cast, arranged by the manager, Mr. Frederick Gye, from a suspicion lest the gay artlessness of the page should in some of the scenes absorb the attention of the public to the disadvantage of the Countess's maid. Sontag as " Susanna " was once in like manner threatened by the rivalry of an almost too attractive " Cherubino ; " but she conjured the danger by entering heart and soul into the impish pleasantries of the playful,. amorous youth.

Madame Lucca was very admirable in the great dramatic parts of " Valentine " and of " Selika." But her grace, her coquettishness, her *espièglerie* (to borrow from the French language a word which has scarcely an equivalent in our own) gave to the part of " Cherubino," and in a less degree to that of " Zerlina," a charm which would be vainly looked for in the impersonations of any other artist.

Madame Lucca terminated her first London engagement, contracted for several years, by an abrupt departure. Her sudden flight was never explained ; not, at least, to the public.

It exposed the fugitive to the payment of a heavy indemnity, as stipulated in the agreement. But when, some years afterwards, the opportunity of re-engaging Madame Lucca presented itself, the manager, putting aside all question of damages and fines, was only too glad to profit by it.

In the year 1870 Madame Lucca appeared as " Leonora " in *La Favorita*, a simple dramatic part presenting none of the variety of light and shade which gives such interest to the personage of " Margherita." The " Leonora " of *La Favorita*, like her namesake of the *Trovatore*, is serious from beginning to end. She is not much better, not much worse, morally speaking, than " Vio-

letta" of *La Traviata;* while there is this to be
said against her, that she is never lively. To be
sure, the dramatist has given her neither the excitement of diamonds, as in the case of " Margherita,"
nor of champagne, as in that of " Violetta ; "
and poor gloomy "Leonora" only once becomes
thoroughly animated when the prospect of death
and the influence of love, stronger than death,
combine to produce in her that " exaltation " which
gives such beauty and such dignity to her final
scene. In this scene, of which it would not be
enough to say that it is worth all the rest of the
opera, Madame Lucca shows herself thoroughly
penetrated with the spirit of the situation, and in
the closing duet attains the highest point of tragic
and pathetic expression. Of course she is very
charming in the duet of the first act ; of course she
sings the grand air of the third, " O mio Fernando,"
with all necessary feeling ; but it is not until the
highly dramatic scene which terminates the opera
that, like the composer of the work, she reveals
herself in all her power.

Madame Lucca, by the nature of her dramatic
talent, is, perhaps, more fitted for the representation of light than of serious parts. With a vivid
impression of her " Margherita " still upon us,
we must nevertheless say that she is seen to
more advantage as " Zerlina " in *Fra Diavolo,* and

above all as " Cherubino " in the *Marriage of Figaro.*
Yet of characters in which lightness, prettiness, and
grace are the chief dramatic essentials these are the
only two which have yet been undertaken by
Madame Lucca.   Many indeed are the qualities
which Madame Lucca possesses.   But her chief
quality of all is " verve ; " a combination of nerve
and spirit, which she possesses to a greater degree
than almost any other vocalist.

When the war of 1870 broke out more than one
prima donna was affected by it.   The Marquis de
Caux, at that time husband of Madame Adelina
Patti, was not in the military service—he had
begun life as a diplomatist, and afterwards held an
appointment in the household of the Empress
Eugénie.   Neither was M. Auguste Rouzaud, husband elect of Madame Christine Nilsson.   He was a
stockbroker, but he was also a mighty hunter ; and
when the war broke out he joined the army of
Paris as a volunteer and took part in several sorties.
Both Madame Lucca's husbands were warriors.
Both served in the Prussian cavalry, and both took
part in the famous charge of Mars la Tour, delivered
August 16, 1870, with the object (duly attained) of
arresting the march of Bazaine's army towards
Paris until German troops should have assembled
in sufficient force to drive back the French up to,
and within the walls of Metz.   Moreover, in this
famous charge both Madame Lucca's husbands

were severely wounded; and both were lying in this condition at one of the numerous hospitals established near Metz, when the intrepid prima donna resolved to visit Baron von Rhaden. She is said to have also visited his intimate friend and destined successor, when from her first husband she had been liberated, not by French bullets, but by American lawyers.

The German newspapers published long and enthusiastic accounts of Madame Lucca's expedition to the neighbourhood of Metz; and one enterprising writer issued in pamphlet form what was represented as a complete narrative of the adventurous journey. The presence of a prima donna in an occupied district was certainly an incident of no ordinary kind. The favourite Court singer of the Emperor William, the fascinating artist who had enjoyed the honour of being photographed together with the illustrious Bismarck (the outcome of a jocular proposition on the part of the vocalist, jocularly accepted by the Minister), had, of course, no trouble in obtaining the necessary passes; and equally as a matter of course she was received wherever she appeared with the utmost attention on the part of the military authorities.

The circumstances under which Madame Lucca obtained her divorce are sufficiently curious to be mentioned. They are known to the present writer from full reports of the proceedings published at the time in the New York papers, and they were briefly as follows :—

Madame Lucca, or rather the Baroness von Rhaden, applied for the dissolution of her marriage with the Baron von Rhaden, on the ground of his infidelity; and on evidence sworn by Madame Lucca, without any opportunity of reply being given to the defendant in the case, the plaintiff's demand was granted. Then Madame Lucca married her second husband, Baron von Wallhofen. A few weeks afterwards, as soon as there was time, a declaration arrived from Baron von Rhaden denying absolutely Madame Lucca's statements as to his infidelity. But the Court, after receiving the evidence proffered by Baron von Rhaden, rejected it, or rather took no action upon it, for the sufficient reason that since the first hearing of the case Madame Lucca, profiting by the decree of divorce, had married a second time.

General considerations apart, it is gratifying to know that the decision of the American tribunal did no harm to any of the parties concerned; not even to Baron von Rhaden, for though, according to his affidavit, he had had no too friendly relations with the young lady against whom his wife's jealousy seem to have been excited, he, nevertheless, as soon as he was at liberty to do so, married her.

It has been said that Madame Lucca was born in

the same year as Adelina Patti and Christine Nilsson; and there seems but little reason for expecting a successor to either of the three.

Madame Lucca began her career as prima donna at Olmütz in 1859 as "Valentine" in *Les Huguenots;* Madame Adelina Patti came out at the Royal Italian Opera of London in 1861 as "Amina" in *La Sonnambula;* and Madame Christine Nilsson made her *début* at the Théâtre Lyrique of Paris in 1864 as "Violetta" in *La Traviata.*

As operatic composers have disappeared it seems in accordance with the fitness of things that singers equal to the interpretation of their works should also disappear. Rossini had scarcely retired when he was replaced by Donizetti and Bellini, and when Donizetti composed his last operas, in 1843, Verdi had already brought out, in 1842, *Nabucco* and *I Lombardi.* For many years past, however, the operatic theatres of Europe have not depended for new works upon Italian composers alone. Verdi's period of activity came to an end in 1859 with *Un ballo en Maschera;* though this did not prevent him from producing twelve years afterwards one of his finest works, *Aida,* and, eighteen years afterwards, *Otello.*

In 1859, just as Verdi virtually retired, Gounod produced an opera which was destined, like so many of those produced by the four leading Italian com-

posers of the last seventy-five years, to acquire a sort
of international character; to be played, that is to
say, in every country, and to be translated into every
language.   When it became evident that the composer of *Faust* had finished his operatic career, the
operas of Wagner all at once became popular: *Lohengrin, Tannhaüser,* and the *Flying Dutchman* passing
into the Italian language, which for musical purposes
is an international tongue; passing also into the
languages of England and of France, though, owing
to the prejudices and, it may be added, the wounded
feelings of the French, Wagner is still excluded
from the French stage, and in the French language
is to be heard only in Belgium.   The lamented
Bizet with his one delightful work; Gounod with
Faust; Wagner with *Lohengrin;* Meyerbeer with *Les
Huguenots, Le Prophète, L'Africaine,* and *Dinorah;*
the four Italian composers who kept the opera of
their country alive from the time of Rossini to that
of Verdi; and finally Mozart with the immortal
Marriage of Figaro, Don Giovanni, and *Magic Flute;*
these are the masters of all nations, and of many
periods, these are the works that are now comprised in the repertory of a so-called Italian Opera,
when organized on the completest scale.   It can be
seen at a glance that of the composers named two
only are living, each of whom has written his last
opera.

CHAPTER VI.

MADAME CHRISTINE, or rather Christina, Nilsson, the second of the "nightingales" given to us by Sweden, with Jenny Lind as first, and Miss Sigrïd Arnoldson, it may be, as third, was born a child of wonder. Seventh child of a seventh child, she was, according to Swedish belief, which in the case of Christine Nilsson can scarcely be treated as a superstition, predestined for great things. That she was the seventh born of a seventh born I have heard from her own lips, though M. Guy de Charnacé, in his " Etoiles du Chant," places her eighth and last in the long list of her brothers and sisters. He also connects her with an interesting national tradition, and assures us that her father in his dreams used to see her surrounded by all kinds of earthly and heavenly glories. In her own native village a story was current of a peasant girl who had become a

queen; and her own native province, that of
Wärend, was the legendary scene of an exploit by
which the fair-haired Blaenda raised herself from
the humblest to the loftiest position.

It may be that the story of Jael and Sisera, compli-
cated with that of Judith and Holofernes, got somehow multiplied and transformed into a Scandinavian
saga. This, in any case, is what the *sagas* tell of
the heroic Blaenda, who, by means which the sweet-
voiced and doubtless tender-hearted Christina would
have shrunk from practising, raised herself to the
rank of " first lady " among the ladies of her country
and of her time.

Sweden had been invaded by the Danes. Then
Blaenda invited the chiefs of the Danish army to a
banquet, where she assembled the most beautiful and
most courageous young women of the neighbourhood. Unable to refuse the insidious drinks presented to them with soft words by smiling maidens,
the reckless warriors found themselves after a time
in a helpless condition; and it may be that meanwhile the wine poured into these maidens' cups
became, by such a miracle as is performed in the
Isaias of Signor Marcinelli, changed into water. In
any case Blaenda and her brave companions remained
self-possessed when the Danish chiefs had already
lost their senses. Then Blaenda drew from beneath
her garments a sickle and cut off the head of the

principal leader, while the other young girls followed her example, each operating on the neck of her particular admirer.

The analogy between the story of Blaenda and that of Christina is not a very striking one. But for lovers of analogies it exists; and, like Blaenda, Christina from a peasant girl became a queen—a Queen of Song.

But it has been said that Christina, besides being a seventh child, was the seventh of a seventh; which makes her miraculous career no longer a marvel.

Patti's parents were both connected with the opera, one of them being a famous singer; and in many cases the natural gifts of a great vocalist have been an hereditary possession. Such, however, was not the case with Christine Nilsson—to give her the forename which, during her residence in France, she was finally to adopt; nor, indeed, with her illustrious predecessor, Jenny Lind. The latter had the good fortune at a very early age to attract the notice of an operatic artist who chanced to hear her sing; and the same thing happened about the same age to Christine Nilsson.

Christine Nilsson was born Aug. 3, 1843, the same year (it has already been said) as Patti and Lucca. One of her brothers, Carl by name, had become a violinist; in which character he used to visit the fairs of the neighbourhood, even at

some considerable distance from the parental
home.   One day, when little Christine was still a
child, the brother found that she was in the habit,
during his absence, of making experiments with his
violin; and that she had already learnt to play upon
the instrument with considerable skill.   Gradually it struck the brother that with the aid of his
sister he might turn his solos into duets; and
soon the little girl made her first appearance at any
fair.

A magistrate, in whom the habit of trying
petty offences had not obliterated all sense of art,
was present at one of Christine Nilsson's performances; and so struck was he by her brilliant talent
that he offered to secure for her a thorough musical
education.   Then it seems to have been that the
father was visited by the dream already mentioned.
But somehow it did not convince him that he would
do well to accept the propositions made to him by the
worthy justice.   The propositions were, however,
repeated in a pressing manner; and in the end
father Nilsson, fortunately for all lovers of music,
gave way, and little Christine became a member of
the magistrate's family.   One day a singer of distinction, Mdlle. Valerius, afterwards Baroness of
Leuhusen, visited the house, and in the midst of
an improvised concert expressed her desire to hear
the little peasant girl of whose charming voice some-

one had spoken to her. Christine sang; and then nothing would satisfy Mdlle. Valerius but to take her away to her own house and there give her regular music lessons. The little girl made much progress under the instruction of Mdlle. Valerius. But it was necessary to teach her other things besides music and singing; and she was now old enough to be sent to school. The next two years she spent at Gottenberg, where she received the rudiments of a good general education. Then the worthy magistrate again took charge of her; and she went with him to Stockholm, where he placed her under the care of an eminent professor and composer, Mr. Franz Berwald. She soon regained all she had lost during her two years of general study; and she now made great progress, not only as a singer, but also as a pianist. The reputation left at Stockholm by Jenny Lind is said to have stimulated her to great exertions. She, in any case, studied with surprising success; and already projects of a "first appearance in public" were entertained. Just then a sister of Mdlle. Valerius, who possessed much talent as a portrait painter, was about to visit Paris. She suggested that Christine should accompany her; and it was soon arranged that the young painter and the still younger singer should go to Paris together. Christine took with her a letter of introduction to an English lady, Madame Collinet, and in Madame Collinet's family she remained some time.

Christine's chief object in going to Paris was to place herself under a good professor; and at Madame Collinet's she made the acquaintance of one of the most successful singing masters of his time, M. Wartel, teacher of Madame Trebelli.

M. Wartel saw at once that Christine's talent fitted her above all for the operatic stage; but his young pupil was timid and had no particular inclination for a theatrical life. One evening, however, she heard Madame Miolan-Carvalho at the Théâtre Lyrique in *La Reine Topaze;* and there was something in the performance of that charming vocalist which told Mdlle. Nilsson that she also was a singer. She informed M. Wartel of the change her ideas had undergone; and now, far from hesitating, she was only anxious that the director of the Théâtre Lyrique, M. Carvalho, should give her a hearing. This was soon arranged by M. Wartel; and a three years' engagement was offered to the young artist, by which she was to receive 2,000 francs a month for the first year, 2,500 for the second, and 3,000 for the third. On the 27th October, 1864, Mdlle. Nilsson, then 21 years of age, made her first appearance.

Historians differ—even operatic historians; and though M. Guy de Charnacé leads us to believe that M. Carvalho was the first director with whom Mdlle.

Nilsson ever treated, Mr. Maurice Strakosch, in his
"Mémoires d'un Impresario," assures us that before
singing at M. Carvalho's theatre Mdlle. Nilsson
accepted an engagement from Eugenio Merelli, son
of the manager who was at that time directing the
Scala of Milan and the Imperial Theatre of Vienna.
Merelli, according to Strakosch, engaged Nilsson
for five years; but though he had the greatest
confidence in her talent, could find nothing for
her to do. Merelli, moreover (always according
to Strakosch), considered that in spite of Mdlle.
Nilsson's talent and charm as a vocalist, he had
committed rather an imprudent action in engaging
her for opera, seeing that she had never appeared
on the stage.

Some days afterwards Merelli met Strakosch
again and told him that his engagement with
Mdlle. Nilsson was at an end. He was glad, he
said, to be obliged no longer to pay her 1,000
francs a month for doing nothing; and Mdlle.
Nilsson must also have been glad, since by her
engagement with M. Carvalho she was to receive
2,000 francs a month.

Mdlle. Nilsson came out at the Théâtre Lyrique
as "Violetta" in a French translation of Verdi's
Traviata; and she did so without much success.
This opera had in like manner failed on its first production at Naples.

At Naples the *fiasco* was caused by a striking want of harmony between the representative of "Violetta" and the "Violetta" who should have been represented. The latter is dying of consumption. The former was excessively robust, so that when the doctor of the piece said, in sorrowful tones, "She is fading away!" the audience, seeing that their "Violetta" was still enormous, could not restrain their laughter.

At the Théâtre Lyrique *La Traviata*, or *Violetta*, as the work was now called, did not meet with the success that might have been expected from the rapturous manner in which the vivacious and charming Piccolomini had been received in the part of the unfortunate heroine at the Théâtre des Italiens. For the French version recalled too strongly to the public the novel and the play from which the subject is taken. For analogous reasons a Shakespearian opera has but little chance of succeeding with the English public. *La Dame aux Camélias*, in its dramatic shape, is called by its author a " comedy ; " and the novel from which the comedy is derived is like the comedy, a picture of contemporary manners. The novel and the play contain, all the same, some highly dramatic scenes, ending with a really pathetic catastrophe.

The dramatic scenes and the catastrophe were alone required by Verdi and his librettist. The

character-painting, the satire of Dumas' novel and
of Dumas' comedy were naturally absent from the
opera, constructed on the same dramatic theme;
and this was not what the public had expected. The
work produced no favourable impression ; and it was
not until Mdlle. Nilsson appeared in her second part,
that of " Astrafiammante," the Queen of Night,
in Mozart's *Magic Flute* that she made a really brilliant success. Mdlle. Nilsson's impersonation of
" Astrafiammante " took the Parisians by storm, or,
to use a more appropriate word, enchanted them.
" Like a true daughter of the North ; like a sister of
Jenny Lind," wrote M. Blaze de Bury, " Christine
Nilsson has entered into the master's idea. If her
clear and resonant voice scales the heavens it is to
curse from on high like a daughter of the Titans.
The notes spring from her mouth like fiery serpents.
She has the laugh-rattle of a Hecate."

The *Magic Flute,* which one would scarcely have
looked upon beforehand as a work likely to please
the French, delighted them. It obtained such a
" run " as scarcely any opera in France had met with
before. Mdlle. Nilsson's next impersonation was to
be even more successful ; and here those who believe
that the French can appreciate and enjoy nothing
but what is light and superficial will say that her
success was quite natural.   The part she now undertook was that of " Martha " in Flotow's ever popular

work. Flotow—"Flotow Magico," as some unscru-
pulous friend is said to have called him—had already
put his favourite subject through no less than three
transformations, when in 1865 he presented *Martha*
to the manager of the Théâtre Lyrique in yet a
fourth.

Count Frederick von Flotow, to judge by the
various forms and the different languages in which
he caused *Martha* to be produced, must have possessed a truly international mind. It was, perhaps,
for that reason that his Mecklenburghian father
wished him to enter the Austrian diplomatic service.
Called upon, at last, to choose between diplomacy
and arms, " he returned," says one of his biographers,
" an evasive answer, and became a composer." He
studied at Paris under Reicha, and, born in 1812,
was scarcely of age when he brought out his first
opera, *Peter and Catherine*, which was performed by
a company of amateurs at the Hotel Castellan.

" After trying his hand once or twice more upon
amateurs," says the biographer already cited, " he
felt almost ready to meet the public at an open
theatre. By way of transition he had recourse to
the Poles, whose misfortunes have been made the
pretext of so many performances ; and in 1840 he
produced an opera called *La Duchesse de Guise*,
which was played at the Salle Ventadour for the
benefit of the Polish exiles." After three or four

not very successful works performed at the Renaissance and at the Opéra Comique, he made his first great hit at Hamburg with *Stradella,* a very melodious work, based upon the famous though mythical scene between Stradella and the assassins who, paid to put him to death, chanced to hear him sing and were unable to slay him by reason of his beautiful voice. *Stradella* was succeeded by *L'Ame en Peine,* composed for the Grand Opera of Paris, and there performed with moderate success. Flotow's German opera, *Stradella,* and his French opera, *L'Ame en Peine,* have both been translated into English; and *Stradella* has also passed into Italian. But Flotow's fate in life was apparently to produce one thoroughly successful international work; and this with *Martha* he really accomplished.

Already, in 1843, Flotow had joined two French composers, MM. Burgmüller and Delvedez, in writing the music of a ballet called *Lady Henriette ou le Marché de Richmond,* which, after being successfully produced at the Grand Opera of Paris, was played in London under the title of *Lady Henrietta; or, the Statute Fair.* On the subject of the ballet, Flotow caused a German libretto to be written; and this, after setting it to music, he called *Martha.* He had adorned his work by introducing in the principal situation the beautiful " Last Rose of Summer;" and with this rose in his button-hole Flotow will doubtless go—at least a little way—down to posterity.

In arranging *Martha* for the Italian stage, the composer added two new airs, one for the contralto, the other for the baritone ; and he made some further changes in arranging it for the Théâtre Lyrique, where, thanks in a great measure to Mdlle. Nilsson's charming impersonation of the heroine, it was represented for upwards of 300 nights. In the German piece the action takes place in the reign of Queen Anne. The author of the Italian version has, for some inscrutable reason, gone back to the fifteenth century. The characters, therefore, in the Italian *Martha* ought, one and all, to wear mediæval costumes; though the heroine invariably attires herself according to the latest fashion. In the French version the librettist has made the incidents of the drama occur almost in the present day.

The ever-to-be-lamented Bosio had already sung the part of " Martha " in the most charming manner at the Royal Italian Opera; and Adelina Patti had achieved as " Martha," at the same theatre, one of her most brilliant successes when Mdlle. Nilsson undertook the character in the new French version at the Théâtre Lyrique.

At the end of her three years' engagement with M. Carvalho, Mdlle. Nilsson went to the Grand Opera ; where, besides appearing as " Marguerite " in

Gounod's *Faust,* she "created" the part of "Ophe-lia" in M. Ambroise Thomas's *Hamlet.*

Hamlet, except in the pretty ballet music and the really poetical scene of Ophelia's death, is the work of a man who is perpetually urging himself to be solemn and sad when nature created him light and cheerful. Our opera-going public, for the most part, knows nothing of Shakespeare, and consequently is not shocked by the terrible absurdities of which the operatic *Hamlet* is full. But in itself, apart from what it suggests, M. Thomas's music is very depress-ing. The *Romeo and Juliet* of M. Gounod, who first taught M. Thomas the art of marrying feeble music to immortal verse, is far preferable to *Hamlet,* in-asmuch as M. Gounod does not think it necessary to make unnatural exertions with the view of raising himself to the level of his poet. All he feels called upon to do is to write as his nature prompts him; and the result is that, though M. Gounod's music is no more Shakespearian than that of M. Thomas, it is at least spontaneous, and possesses some *naïveté*—a quality in which M. Thomas's high pressure strains are wholly wanting.

The time had now come for Mdlle. Nilsson to sing in London; and in 1867, being on a visit at the house of Mr. Vivian, she appeared under Mr. Maple-son's management at Her Majesty's Theatre, where she played successively all the parts in which she had distinguished herself at the Théâtre Lyrique and the Grand Opera, with the exception only of " Ophelia;" for the opera of *Hamlet* had been secured by Mr. Gye for Covent Garden Theatre, where the principal part was played with but moderate success by the fair-haired Mdlle. Sessi. The comparative failure of the work was owing to no fault of Mdlle. Sessi's, but to the pretentiousness and dulness of the opera.

It is now more than twenty years since Mdlle. Nilsson sang for the first time on the Anglo-Italian boards. On the 8th of June, 1867, before a public which had not yet forgotten the "Violetta" of Mdlle. Piccolomini, a new "Violetta" came forward and at once took the hearts of all who heard her. Indeed, the very appearance of Mdlle. Nilsson when she advanced to sing her "brindisi," with its accompaniment of champagne, caused a murmur of applause which must have at once set the fair *débutante* at rest as to the impression she had already made on the English public. It soon became manifest that the charm of her voice and singing was as great as that of her person and demeanour. Before she had finished the first verse of "Libiamo" she was already accepted as a public favourite; and at the conclusion of the opera she was applauded, called and recalled with a fervour such as is never awakened but by a really great singer.

Mdlle. Piccolomini, it is true, had been applauded with rapture at the same theatre; but the very charm of Mdlle. Nilsson's performance lay in the contrast it presented to the passionate realism of her impulsive predecessor. She refined to the utmost a character sadly in want of refinement, and sang in absolute perfection the expressive music of the part. Her "Violetta" never went into hysterics; and she seemed to die, not of phthisis aided and developed by dissipation, but of a broken heart, like Clarissa Harlowe or like that Shakespearian maiden who "never told her love." Mdlle. Piccolomini's "Violetta" was a foolish virgin; Mdlle. Nilsson's a fallen angel.

So profound was the first impression made by Mdlle. Nilsson in *La Traviata* that when some years later, after her return from America, she essayed a more dramatic, more realistic rendering of the part, everyone objected to the new "Violetta" that this was not the "Violetta" to which Mdlle. Nilsson had originally introduced us.

Mdlle. Nilsson's next impersonation at Her Majesty's Theatre was "Margherita" in *Faust*, a character thoroughly in harmony with her poetic temperament. It was observed that in the first scenes the new "Margherita's" costume was closely copied from the well-known figure of "Gretchen" by Ary Scheffer; and if Scheffer had been alive and had wished to illustrate the drama throughout, he might in every scene have taken Mdlle. Nilsson for the model of his heroine. Of all the Margheritas—lively and coquettish Margheritas, sombre and impassioned Margheritas, Margheritas of every description— none more naïve, more innocent could be seen than the " Margherita " presented by Mdlle. Nilsson.

In some respects Mdlle. Nilsson's " Margherita " resembled the " Margherita " of Madame Miolan-Carvalho, for whom the part was written. But Mdlle. Nilsson's "Margherita" was the more natural of the two. Madame Miolan-Carvalho's " Margherita" moved about the stage with fixed attitudes and looks, as though in a prolonged fit of somnambulism.

As to the singing, Mdlle. Nilsson's voice seemed now, more than ever, remarkable for its purity of tone ; while such was the perfection of her execution that the sentimental spinning song, the brilliant air of the jewels, and the melody in which "Margherita " gives so touching an account of her little sister's illness and death, were all sung with equal, and that the very greatest, effect.

The third character assumed by Mdlle. Nilsson in England was that of " Martha," in which she had appeared some three hundred times at the Théâtre Lyrique. It was easy to understand why Mdlle. Nilsson had played the part so often in Paris. Her " Martha " was indeed a charming impersonation ;

while the "Last Rose of Summer," as given by her, was a happy example of a thoroughly beautiful melody sung with perfect expression by a thoroughly beautiful voice. About this time Mdlle. Nilsson made her first appearance at the Philharmonic Concerts, when she sang the second of "Astrafiammante's" solos in the *Zauberflöte*. Never before (except, perhaps, by the original representative of the Queen of Night) had "Gli angui d'inferno" been sung with such genuine expression, such brilliant effect. The concert audience found, as was afterwards discovered by oratorio audiences, that the opera public had, as usual, been right in its judgment. In fact, so varied are the demands made upon a singer in opera, that a thoroughly successful opera singer is sure to succeed in every style.

After appearing with the most distinguished success as "Violetta," "Margherita," and "Martha," Mdlle. Nilsson now undertook the usually neglected part of "Donna Elvira" in *Don Giovanni;* which, as previously at the Théâtre Lyrique, she at once brought into prominence. The lamentations of this ill-used lady are not, as a rule, thought to form the most interesting part of Mozart's opera. But with Mdlle. Nilsson in the character, "Elvira," instead of being wearisome with her perpetual plaints, became highly interesting. The audience heard with sympathy her tales of woe, and felt that to deceive, and worse still, abandon so charming a woman was to combine crime with folly. Never did the public entertain so bad an opinion of " Don Juan" as when the part of " Elvira," to whose engaging appeals he listens unmoved, was played by Mdlle. Nilsson.

Mdlle. Nilsson's success in the four parts just named was so great that if success in the plainest sense of the word had been her only object, she might well have abstained from assuming any others. But not to confine herself to repetitions, and as if to show the wideness of her dramatic range, she appeared in successive seasons as the sad, sentimental " Lucia," and as the arch and amorous " Cherubino." Mdlle. Nilsson is one of the two or three living artists who enjoy not only a European but a world-wide reputation ; and by London audiences she has always been held in the very highest esteem. Moscow and St. Petersburg know her as well as New York ; London knows her better even than Paris, where she made her first studies and her first appearance on the stage, but where she has never to this moment been heard in Italian Opera. Now not to have heard Mdlle. Nilsson in Italian Opera is to have missed one important side of her very complete talent. In London she has appeared in all the characters which she had made her own years before at the Théâtre Lyrique ; and she has also sung a remarkably large number of Italian parts.

She made her *début*, as already mentioned, in the character of ": Violetta," and had a prominent place at once assigned to her in that interesting class of vocalists known as " light soprani." There are some singers, no doubt, to whom this designation may be fitly applied—singers with high, thin, flexible voices capable of executing florid music in brilliant style, but not equally capable of giving due expression to music of a grave and emotional character. Formerly no such distinction as that now recognized between the " light soprano " and the " dramatic soprano " was known.

Meyerbeer, as previously pointed out, was the first composer who wrote systematically for the two kinds of soprano voice ; as, for example, in *Les Huguenots*, which contains one soprano part of a highly dramatic cast and one of a purely ornamental kind. In the days of Pasta, Malibran, and Sontag every soprano sang every kind of music written for the soprano voice. But the airs and passages given to " Valentine " are so different from those assigned to " Marguerite de Valois " that one can scarcely think of any singer who could render full justice to both characters. Neither, however, is beyond the means of Mdlle. Nilsson, who is equally perfect as " Astrafiammante " in the *Magic Flute*, and as " Leonora " in *Il Trovatore*, and who certainly could sing the music of both the soprano parts in

Les Huguenots. It is only in one of them, however, that she has been heard—and in the very one which some years since would have been considered quite unsuited to her talent. Yet her "Valentine" is as admirable an impersonation as her "Desdemona," her "Violetta," or her "Mignon."

In 1869, when Mr. Mapleson and Mr. Gye combined their forces at the Royal Italian Opera, Mdlle. Nilsson appeared in her famous part of "Ophelia." She acted and sang it with infinite grace; but the work was so dull, so dead, that not even Mdlle. Nilsson, with all her inspiration, could breathe into it the breath of life.

The only part which Mdlle. Nilsson has had the opportunity of "creating"—though to many she has given a new character—is that of "Edith" in Balfe's *Talisman*, or *Talismano*; for, composed to an English libretto by the late Arthur Matheson, it was produced in an Italian, or rather an Italianized, version with the spoken dialogue of the original put into recitative. Balfe, thanks to himself and to his own tuneful, singable music, has more than once been fortunate in his singers. In one of his earliest operas, the *Maid of Artois*, the principal part was undertaken by Malibran. In his latest work, produced after his death, the heroine was impersonated by Nilsson. The final rondo of the *Maid of Artois* has been sung by many a famous prima donna. It

became known as " Balfe's air," or " L'air de Balfe"
—as though he had not written a hundred others,
many of them more melodious and more original
than this " L'air de Balfe." When Balfe went for
the first time to St. Petersburg, the Empress Marie
Feodorovna, wife of the Emperor Nicholas, thought
all at once, on his being presented to her, of " L'air
de Balfe," and said to him, " Vous êtes Monsieur
Balfe de l'air ?"

The tenor part in the Italian version of the
Bohemian Girl has been sung at Her Majesty's
Theatre by Giuglini, and the principal air in
that part (much more worthy of being known as
" L'air de Balfe " than the final rondo of the *Maid
of Artois*) by Mario. Balfe's *Falstaff*, moreover, had,
some fifty years ago, the supreme advantage of being
sung by all the best singers then engaged at Her
Majesty's Theatre, with Grisi and Lablache among
them.

In undertaking the part of the heroine in *Il
Talismano* Mdlle. Nilsson fulfilled a promise she had
made to the composer some years before his death.
Presented in its original English form the work
would probably have met with more success than
it obtained in the Italianized version. Balfe's grand
operas, or operas with full recitative, have never
made much impression on the English public. This
was shown in the case of one of his most carefully

written works, *The Bondman,* which is said to have
been received with favour in Germany, but which
in England, owing in a great measure to its being
composed throughout in music, fell flat.

When Mdlle. Nilsson appeared as " Edith Plantagenet" in Balfe's posthumous opera of *Il Talismano,* never did a public favourite, coming back to
the scene of many triumphs, meet with a warmer
reception.   More significant, however, than either
the applause at the beginning of the performance,
or the applause strengthened and adorned by bouquets at the end, was the fact that the newly-arrived
artist had returned in admirable voice.   In the
melodious andante of " Edith's " opening air, " Plo-
cida notte," Mdlle. Nilsson was heard at her best.
She sang the tormented allegro which concludes the
air, and which forms so striking a contrast to the
preceding movement, as it was doubtless intended to
be sung ; and the spirit with which she declaimed the
final passages of the second movement called forth
more applause than even her expressive singing in
the first.   At the end of the opening air, and subsequently on every possible occasion, Mdlle. Nilsson was applauded, recalled, and, on coming back,
received with salvoes of bouquets.   In the grand
duet with the tenor she sang with much dramatic
feeling ; and nothing could have been neater or
more brilliant than her perfect execution of the joy-

ous solo in galop time, which, with its elaborate variations, adorns the last act. How, on the termination of the opera, Mdlle. Nilsson was once more called before the curtain to receive the plaudits of an enthusiastic audience need scarcely be told.

The part of the tenor fell to the lot of Signor Campanini, who is, at least, the possessor of a fine voice. It would be difficult just now to name another tenor who can sing passages of sustained notes as firmly and as expressively as Signor Campanini. His only fault is that he is a little too much like the "ignoble fisherman," whose son he imagines himself to be, when he assumes the part of " Gennaro" in *Lucrezia Borgia.* His singing of the pretty air "Candido fiore" left nothing to be desired; and if in " Sir Kenneth's " more pretentious, and more lugubrious solo (second act) he produced a less favourable impression, that was the fault, not of the singer, but of the song. In the duet with " Edith," and generally throughout the opera, Signor Campanini was excellent.

A new baritone, Signor Galassi, but for the English malady of hoarseness from which so many of our foreign visitors suffer, would have been as successful in the part of " Richard " as he had previously been in those of " Rigoletto " and " Figaro " (*Le Nozze*). He at least sang with those " good intentions " which, however little they may be worth in morals, are of indisputable value in art; and but for a voice made rebellious by the London weather, would have obtained excellent results. As it was, he delivered "Richard's" prayer very finely; and in the martial and more or less Verdi-like allegro, which follows the prayer as action should follow meditation, he roused the audience to the warmest expressions of admiration. This sonorous air and chorus ought to have brought the second act to a conclusion. After such an outburst of bravery and brass instruments no further effect can be produced, and the curtain should come down.

As "Queen Berengaria" Madame Marie Roze sang in perfection the slightly quaint, very pretty, and, above all, very original romance assigned to that lady.

No work of Balfe's had ever before enjoyed such advantages as were given to *Il Talismano* at Her Majesty's Opera. The same composer's *Maid of Artois* did, it is true, contain a part written expressly for Malibran, as that of "Edith Plantagenet" was written expressly for Mdlle. Nilsson. It has been said, too, that Balfe's *Falstaff* was composed for the Italian company of Her Majesty's Theatre, or King's Theatre, as it was at that time called. *Falstaff* did not, in any case, meet with so much success as *Il Talismano*, which seemed to appeal equally to the lovers of Italian and of English

Opera. The work was well executed by sub-ordinates as well as by principals, though an exception might be made here and there as regards the chorus, which was at times uncertain. The orchestra was perfect, and this is an important point in connection with *Il Talismano*, which has been more carefully instrumented than most of Balfe's operas. In one place the mass of strings is heard in unison, as in *L'Africaine*. In another the tenor sings to the accompaniment of a single viola (which, sing-ing at the very back of the stage, he must find it difficult to hear) as in *Les Huguenots*. But every composer borrows from every other composer; and if in Balfe's last opera there is here something of Meyerbeer, there something of Verdi, there is also a great deal everywhere of Balfe himself.

No account of Mdlle. Nilsson's performances would be complete without some mention of her very poetical, very dramatic impersonation of " Elsa " in *Lohengrin*. Mdlle. Nilsson, however, has taken no part in popularizing the music of Wagner beyond her admirable performance in his best known work.

This sketch of Mdlle. Nilsson's distinguished career having been begun with a brief account of her family in Sweden, must not be ended without a record of the fact that the first money she saved was expended in purchasing farms for her parents and for one of her brothers. When in due time she paid a visit to her native land, it may be imagined with what enthusiasm she was received. Nothing like it had been seen since the time of Jenny Lind.

Her first appearance among the friends of her youth was marked by an interesting incident. A village ball was going on, and all the young men were eager to dance with the visitor from another and greater world, who yet, by former associations, as by still existing sympathies, belonged to them.

"I cannot dance with you all, but I can play to you all," said the prima donna, who, in early days, had been a violinist; and, taking up the violin, she played Swedish national dances with all the expression and all the fire with which she sings Swedish national songs.

A visit to America is now an event in the life of every famous prima donna; and Mdlle. Nilsson has made more than one American tour, and always with the greatest possible success. Once, moreover, in her life the prima donna, as a rule, gets married; and Mdlle. Nilsson, like Madame Patti and Madame Lucca (but in a more regular manner), has been married twice. Her first husband was M. Auguste Rouzaud (nephew of Admiral Rouzaud), a capital shot and an amiable, gentlemanly man. Stockbroker by occupation, and sportsman by taste, he succeeded more in the latter than in the former character. He killed large game in America, and served with distinction in the army of Paris during the siege; but he came to grief on the Paris Bourse. It must be mentioned in connection with Mdlle. Nilsson's first marriage that it was celebrated at Westminster Abbey (1872); Dean Stanley, who was a friend of the bride, performing the service.

Some years after the death of M. Rouzaud, whose end was hastened by mental distress consequent on his heavy losses, Madame Nilsson married early in 1887 a Spanish nobleman, Count de Miranda; and she has not since her second marriage appeared either in the concert room or on the stage.

CHAPTER VII.

ALBANI.

THE family name of Madame Albani is, or rather was, Lajeunesse; which would seem to denote that she is not of Italian but of French origin. Italian by voice, style, and musical education, this charming singer is by birth a French Canadian. She is sometimes claimed as belonging to the United States. But while she is partly Italian, partly French, and on the ground of a few years' residence in the United States may be looked upon as in some degree American, there can be no mistake as to her being, in at least one important respect, English. As a Canadian she was born an English subject. As the wife of Mr. Ernest Gye, she is an English subject by marriage. Her first, greatest, and most permanent success, moreover, was gained in England. The Royal Italian Opera-house was the first important theatre at which Mdlle. Albani sang; and it

is the only one at which she has sung continuously
year after year.   Mdlle. Albani made her first appearance at Covent Garden in 1871, and since then
she has undertaken a remarkably large number of
Italian parts, belonging, for the most part, to the
" light soprano " class; besides such characters, in
French Opera, as the " Marguerite " of Gounod
and the " Mignon " and " Ophelia " of Ambroise
Thomas, together with several Wagnerian impersonations, which, previously, no Italian singer had
undertaken.   Indeed, to this moment Mdlle. Albani
is the only Italian artist who has appeared as " Elsa "
in *Lohengrin,* as " Elizabeth " in *Tannhaüser,* and as
" Senta " in the *Flying Dutchman.*   Apart from her
own characteristic personal qualities, the fact of
Mdlle. Albani having identified herself with these
creations of the great German composer would alone
suffice to give her a particular distinction among
Italian artists.

Nothing, indeed, can be more graceful or more
poetical than Mdlle. Albani's " Elsa."   Her performance of this part is marked by so much sponta-
neity, so much naturalness, that seeing it one forgets
that " Elsa " is, unhappily, not the sort of maiden
to be met with in this world.   She belongs to
the world of legends and ballads to which one may
be transported in a dream, or, with more certainty,
by a fine representation of *Lohengrin,* with Mdlle.

Albani in the character of the heroine. Without "creating" the part in the ordinary sense
of the word, Mdlle. Albani did not, as "Elsa,"
follow in the track of any other artist; which she
could scarcely avoid doing when she appeared as
" Amina," as " Elvira," as "Lucia," and as "Gilda."
Nor as " Margherita " did she by any means shine
alone, though she at once gained for herself a place
among two or three " Margheritas " of the first rank.
Mdlle. Albani's " Margherita " is a very poetical
conception, with a poetry of the elegiac rather than
of the dramatic kind. Her impersonation, indeed, is
marked by a distinctness and individuality which
serves for the time being to make us forget all other
" Margheritas " for the one before us.

It was not, however, as " Margherita," nor, as a
matter of course, was it in any of the Wagnerian
parts that Mdlle. Albani achieved her first success
at the Royal Italian Opera. Her first success
coincided with her first appearance; and, like
Madame Patti and Mdlle. Gerster, Mdlle. Albani
made her *début* as " Amina " in *La Sonnambula;*
an opera of some years standing, which may yet, in
spite of solemn sneers at its composer's alleged
want of dramatic power, outlive a good many
works of infinitely greater pretensions. Nor was it
in London that Mdlle. Albani first took the
character of " Amina." The scene of her first

appearance in this part, as of her first appearance on any stage, was Messina, in the very country where the action of *La Sonnambula* is supposed to take place, and where the happily inspired composer of that melodious work was born. From Messina Mdlle. Albani reached London by way of Malta, where, arrived in an English possession, she must have already felt herself at home. From Malta to England was, in fact, a far less arduous journey than from the little village of Chamblay, in French Canada, to Messina; for it was at Chamblay, her birthplace, that Mdlle. Albani commenced those studies which ended in making her one of the ablest dramatic artists, and one of the most finished vocalists of our time. Like most singers of real talent, Emma Lajeunesse sang as a child; and she had the advantage of receiving, at a very early age, from her father, a professor of music, lessons on the piano and on the harp. In the midst of her vocal studies she has never neglected the piano; and one of the first of our modern pianists has been heard to speak with unqualified approbation of her performance on the instrument of his choice. Musical talent is apparently an inheritance in the Lajeunesse family, for Mdlle. Albani has a sister who has studied the piano with great success at one of the great German academies.

From the village of Chamblay Mdlle. Lajeunesse

went at the age of five to Montreal, in the immediate neighbourhood, and there entered the
school of the Sacré Cœur. When on the point of
leaving the convent, she is said to have manifested
a strong desire to adopt a religious life, a wish
which fortunately was not destined to be gratified.

The Superior of the convent, with a discernment
which does her honour, perceived that her promis-
ing pupil was fitted for a more extended sphere
than that within which she proposed to enclose herself ; and, at this lady's earnest recommendation, the
future prima donna abandoned all thought of taking
the veil except as " Lucia," " Elvira," and other
operatic brides. About the year 1864 the Lajeunesse
family left Montreal and went to Albany, the capital of
the State of New York. Here the youthful vocalist,
while pursuing her studies, sang on Sundays in the
choir of the cathedral; and the Metropolitan church
used, it is said, to be attended by crowds of pious
amateurs eager to hear the voice of a singer whose
name was unknown to them, but whose tones, once
heard, could not be forgotten. The fame of the
young Canadian soprano went on increasing; the
crowd of religious connoisseurs became every Sunday
greater and greater; until at last the Bishop of
Albany, with a public spirit equal to that which
had previously been shown by the Superior of the
convent at Montreal, declared that this lofty

talent, this angelic voice, were not for his church alone, but for the whole civilized world. The excellent prelate advised M. Lajeunesse to take his daughter to Europe, and place her under masters capable of developing her voice and of doing justice to her musical aptitude generally. That the good Bishop's counsel might be at once acted upon, a concert was given for the purpose of defraying a portion of the necessary expenditure; and at the earliest opportunity father and daughter left New York for Europe, and, going straight to Paris, called upon Duprez, who had given up singing, and had now become a professor of the art in which he had shown himself practically so great a master.

Mdlle. Lajeunesse studied under Duprez for two years, when, by his advice, she went to the Conservatorio of Milan, bearing a letter of introduction from Duprez to Lamperti, the celebrated professor of singing at that institution. Signor Lamperti received the young aspirant in the most encouraging manner, and at once predicted for her a brilliant future. Mdlle. Lajeunesse studied for some considerable time under Lamperti, to whose instruction the perfection of her style may, in a great degree, be attributed. But if Mdlle. Albani owes much to Signor Lamperti, he on his side is greatly indebted to her. For in this artist's perfect execution the public has an example of what can be produced (given, of course, a voice of remarkable beauty) by a method the merit of which is sometimes discussed. Signor Lamperti is known in any case to regard Mdlle. Albani as an artist of, in some measure, his own creation; and his recently published work on "the shake" is dedicated to this accomplished vocalist, whose shake is, indeed, marvellous—clear, firm, and evenly balanced.

It was not until after the completion of her period of study at Milan that Mdlle. Lajeunesse resolved to appear on the stage. In arriving at this decision she was assisted neither by a nun nor by a Bishop, but by her very judicious professors. Signor Lamperti knew, of course, that there could be nothing dangerous or disagreeable in the life of an operatic artist who, from the very beginning of her career, would take the highest position. When, in 1870, Mdlle. Lajeunesse made her *début* at Messina in the opera of *La Sonnambula*, she assumed, in memory of the cathedral where she had sung, and of the kind-hearted Bishop who had given her such good advice, the name of "Albani;" and it has already been told how, from Messina, she passed to Malta, whence, through the English garrison, some account of her brilliant talent could not but find its way to England. After her first season at the Royal Italian Opera, not quite satisfied with herself—though she had been enthusiastically re-

ceived, and had already taken her place among the
first singers of the day—Mdlle. Albani went back
to Milan and studied once more very assiduously
for several months under her old master. Late in
the winter of 1871 she appeared with remarkable
success at the Pergola Theatre of Florence. Returning to London in 1872, she was in the autumn
of that year engaged for Paris. In 1873, after the
conclusion of the London season, she sang at St.
Petersburg, and before coming to London for the
season of 1874 found time to make a voyage to
New York, where one of the first places she visited
was the Cathedral of Albany, and one of the first
persons the benevolent prelate, to whom all lovers
of music should feel grateful for having persuaded
his charming chorister to adopt the profession which
she had evidently been born to follow, and of which
she now forms one of the brightest ornaments.
Mdlle. Lajeunesse of Chamblay, Mdlle. Albani of
Albany, has at present an English name, and
belongs, not as a Canadian subject alone, to England. But England was not the only country, nor
London the only capital, from which, on the
occasion of her marriage, she received numerous
messages of congratulation.

In England Madame Albani is particularly associated with the heroines of Wagner's operas ; or at
least with two of them, "Elsa" and "Elizabeth;" and

though other "Elsas" have appeared among us, she
was the first vocalist to undertake the part at an
English or Anglo-Italian theatre.   She has kept to
the part, moreover, and has sung it every year—in
Italian generally, but now and then in German—
since a dozen years ago she first undertook it.

It is already interesting to speculate as to the
effect which Wagner's death will have in increasing
or diminishing his fame as a composer.   That he
has made for himself throughout all ages a great
name, both as a musician and as a writer on music,
will scarcely be disputed.   But for the very reason
that he was a powerful writer on all that concerned
his art, that he exercised great personal influence,
and that he was a man of action as much as a man
of thought and of imagination, his disappearance
from the scene on which for some thirty or forty
years he fought so many battles, sustained so
many defeats, and gained so many triumphs, will
possibly have the effect, if not of lessening his reputation, at least of leaving it where it stood.   The
composer, as a rule, is not a man of action; and
Richard   Wagner   was   probably   only   one—certainly the only one of eminence—who ever made
speeches to revolutionary mobs and declared war
against the legitimate Government of his country.
At that time Wagner held that the only hope for art
lay in its appreciation by the masses; though he

rested his expectations in after-days, when fresh opportunities had presented themselves, on the patronage of Kings.

In his youth he worshipped at many shrines; and when, as sometimes happened, the idol did not respond to his adoration, he took up his pen, as the savage takes up a stick, and attacked the unresponsive god. He has himself told the world (for a letter from Wagner was sure at once to be translated into every European language) how as a young man he composed a symphony which he laid before Mendelssohn, and which Mendelssohn seems (scarcely to his credit) to have omitted even to look at; and everyone interested in the facts of Wagner's life knew that in Paris he waited upon Meyerbeer, who treated him with much consideration, but failed at the same time to render him any important service. In after years Mendelssohn and Meyerbeer were the select objects of Wagner's satire and invective.

Meyerbeer—the anticipator of Wagner in some at least of his reforms—was treated by the arch-innovator as a sort of charlatan who, borrowing from every side every species of musical, dramatic, scenic, and spectacular effect, combined the whole in one heterogeneous mass, which, owing its existence to no primal spontaneous idea on the part of the composer, possessed no genuine poetic life; and the story will never, perhaps, be forgotten in Eng-

land of Wagner's preparing himself to conduct one
of Mendelssohn's symphonies at the Philharmonic
Concert by carefully putting on his gloves, as though
to place himself as little as possible in contact with
so debasing a composer. This anecdote is not repeated with any view of perpetuating the memory of
a very fantastic piece of wit, which might as well be
allowed to fall into oblivion; but in order to give
an example of the means adopted by Wagner, when
no others were at hand, for making war upon his
enemies.

In England Wagner was known as a writer on the
theory of opera, and as a fierce assailant of all other
operatic composers, long before any one of his works,
in this country at least, had been performed; and
he went so far as to maintain that his operas were
excluded systematically from our theatres by reason
of the prejudice which the English must naturally,
as readers of the Old Testament and strict
Sabbatarians, entertain against one who was at
open war with Judaism. Very few lovers of music
in England can be supposed to have troubled themselves about the race or religion of Mendelssohn
and Meyerbeer—both of whom, by the way, were
Protestant Christians; and scarcely any could have
read Wagner's tract on "Judaism in Music" at
the time when he was gravely asserting that the
apparent opposition to his music in England arose

from the Judaic sympathies and tendencies of the Scripture-reading, Sabbath-keeping English people.

When, at last, a crusade was undertaken in England on behalf of Wagnerian music, the movement was organized under the authority, if not at the direct suggestion, of Wagner himself. Wagner Societies were founded, of which one had its headquarters in London; and the object of these associations was to give an idea of Wagner's music, so far as that could be done through the presentation of excerpts in concert-rooms; and to make contributions out of the proceeds from the concerts towards the performance of the great Wagnerian trilogy or tetralogy (for the *Ring des Nibelungen,* with its prologue and three parts, goes by both names) which was given for the first time at Bayrenth in 1876. The construction of the Bayrenth Theatre, with a special view to the representations of the *Ring des Nibelungen,* must have cost no small sum; and if the general execution of the enterprise demanded the talent of an organizer, the collection of the Wagnerian revenue called for abilities of the administrative kind, while the preparation of the Wagnerian budget was simply a work of financial genius. Wagner was now at the zenith of his power. The Emperor of Germany was his friend, and the King of Bavaria his slave; intermediate positions being held by the other German Sovereigns, all of whom were allowed to contribute to the immense capital necessary for the production of the great work of the " Master's " life.

Up to the year 1869 not one of the German master's operas had been heard in this country; and such a reputation for being tuneless and tiresome had been made for him that there seemed but little chance of any work of his having so much as a trial given to it at any of our great Opera-houses. *Lohengrin* used, from time to time, to be announced in those fantastic documents known as operatic prospectuses. But no one paid serious attention to the promise of its performance, which by many was regarded as a species of threat; and the announcement at last excited such general derision that the rival directors, as if by common consent, abstained from repeating it.

There were many reasons to render it probable that the *Flying Dutchman*, written in the composer's earliest manner, would be received without any very violent protestations of dislike. *Tannhaüser*, played not many years before at the Grand Opera of Paris, at the express recommendation of the Emperor and under his direct patronage, had been hissed and hooted from the stage. But the *Flying Dutchman* was, even to the most determined opponents of Wagnerism, a comparatively inoffensive work. Much of it is composed in the ancient manner, before the Master had finally convinced himself that the opera of the past was false in principle and foolish in effect, and that the "art work of the future" must be framed on altogther new lines. The *Flying Dutchman* contains what are vulgarly called "tunes;" comparatively melodious airs built more or less in accordance with the ancient methods; duets with passages in which the voices are heard together; and concerted pieces. The "leading motive" system, to receive such prodigious extension in after years, is in this opera scarcely more than indicated by one oft-recurring example. The *Flying Dutchman*, in short, belongs to a period in Wagner's development when, from his own point of view, he was still among the unregenerate; from the point of view of his antagonists, still one of the unperverted.

For English play-goers, moreover, the work had the advantage of being based on a legend, which, whatever its origin, first took literary form in an English tale. The story of the audacious mariner, condemned for his rebellious disposition, and his impious defiance of the laws of nature, to sail eternally and hopelessly from sea to sea, may be known in various countries. But in its first known presentation it is English; and it was in England, and apparently at the Adelphi Theatre, that Heine witnessed the performance of that melodramatic *Flying Dutchman* to which, in his narrative of the representation as preserved in the *Reisebilder*,

he gave the poetic meaning adopted by Wagner in
the libretto for which Heine's fancied and fanciful
recollection of Fitzball's rather commonplace piece
is known to have served as basis. The idea, then, of
producing in the year 1869 one of the least Wagnerian of Wagner's operas was not so wild as,
at the time, it may have seemed. The experiment
was, in any case, justified by the result; and it
might have been thought that, the ice having once
been broken, and Wagner's opera having been found
much more tolerable than had been expected, other
works more decidedly Wagnerian in character would
be produced. But 1870, and again 1871, passed
without any fresh Wagnerian performance; and it
was not until after the close of the Franco-German
war, and as a direct consequence of that struggle,
that Wagnerism, in the form of *Lohengrin*, from
Germany reached Italy, whence, by Campanini,
representing the Knight of the Swan, it was carried
across the Atlantic to New York, to reach England
some months later. The Italians in 1871 felt grateful to the Germans for having enabled them to
establish their government in Rome; and by way of
testifying their gratitude they could think of nothing
better than to produce the most generally admired
work of Germany's great musical composer.

When it was seen in England and in America
that *Lohengrin* could be appreciated by Italian audi-

ences, the belief up to that time cherished that Wagner's operas could not be represented with success outside Germany fell to the ground; and even if Signor Campanini had not borne with him to New York, the armour, the helmet, and better still, the part itself, of the Keeper of the Holy Grail, the favour with which the work had been received in Italy must have sufficed to recommend it for performance in other countries. As in London we seldom do things by halves, *Lohengrin*, when at last our audiences were permitted to hear it, was produced almost simultaneously at both our Opera-houses. Then, although in former years it had been said that, amongst our Italian and Italianized vocalists, we had not one who could undertake with advantage the character of "Elsa," it suddenly appeared that we possessed at least two : at Covent Garden Madame Albani, whose impersonation of "Elsa" was afterwards to gain for her in the Prussian capital the warmest commendations and the highest honours; and at Her Majesty's Theatre Madame Nilsson, whose "Elsa" is only not admired in countries where she has never been seen in that part, so perfectly suited to her voice and style.

Since the great *Lohengrin* year, Wagnerism has spread through the country in all directions; and our audiences have been familiarized by Mr. Gye with

Tannhäuser and by Mr. Carl Rosa with *Rienzi :* that earliest and least Wagnerian of all Wagner's works.

When 1876 arrived, with its Wagner Festival, a taste for Wagnerian music had already affected so many of our amateurs that numbers of musical pilgrims left London to attend the representations of the great Wagnerian cyclus at Bayrenth. Nor must the series of Wagner Concerts given at the Albert Hall under the direction of Wagner himself, and of his faithful lieutenant, Herr Richter, be forgotten.

Herr Richter afterwards parted company with his chief; but only to proclaim his merits, and to conduct his works in other quarters. He it was, moreover, who, some years later, presented to us at Drury Lane, under the management of Mr. Franke, the *Meistersinger* and *Tristan und Isolde.* Then came the production at Her Majesty's Theatre of Wagner's elaborate work, more epic than dramatic, on subjects from the *Nibelungen Lied*, performed twice over in its completeness, but destined to be made thoroughly known to us in its most essential parts and through its greatest beauties, by the orchestral arrangements, and the arrangements for orchestra and voices presented some years later by Herr Richter at his admirable concerts.

The English public, then, has enjoyed the opportunity of hearing everything in the way of dramatic music that Wagner has written. Even *Parsifal*, the master's last work, has been performed in London; though, as presented at the Albert Hall by Mr. Barnby, it was, of course, given without dramatic action—in other words, incompletely.

Madame Albani has played the part of "Elsa" before English audiences both in Italian and in German; and she is the only prima donna who in England has undertaken three different Wagnerian impersonations: those of "Senta," "Elizabeth," and "Elsa."

The part of "Senta" was in England first undertaken by Mdlle. Ilma de Murska, when, in 1869, the *Flying Dutchman* was produced at Drury Lane, under the management of Mr. George Wood; the year in which Mr. Mapleson and Mr. Gye combined their forces at Covent Garden with Titiens, Patti, Lucca, and Albani in the same company.

Madame Albani and Madame Nilsson have both appeared repeatedly as "Elsa."

Mdlle. Titiens has appeared as "Ortrud;" and Mr. Santley was the first representative in England (at Drury Lane in 1869) of the "Flying Dutchman."

At the present time, in the year 1888, the only one of Wagner's operas which can be said to have taken a firm hold on English taste is *Lohengrin ;* and the representations of this work, under Mr.

Carl Rosa, during the season of 1887, with Madame Marie Roze in the part of " Elsa," were always received by crowded audiences with the warmest applause. No more romantic, more poetic work exists in music.

Lohengrin continues to be played in Germany much oftener than any other of Wagner's works. Next in general appreciation to *Lohengrin* stands among the Germans the singularly beautiful *Walkyrie*; the second of the four pieces which together constitute the *Ring des Nibelungen*. In England this work is only known from the two performances of the *Ring* already referred to as having taken place with a German company at Her Majesty's Theatre.

CHAPTER VIII.

A FLIGHT OF PRIME DONNE.

BYRON is of modern poets the best known in the whole world, not by reason of his poetry alone, but also by reason of his adventures. So with prime donne ; those being the most famous who have not only sung admirably, but have also played a dramatic part in life. Many a prima donna, then, to whom I should have been delighted to assign a place in this book, must be kept out or mentioned in only the most casual way, not from any fault of hers, but often from her very merits.

Anastasia Robinson is remembered as one of our leading English vocalists by many who do not know in what operas she sang or what was the character of her voice, but who have heard of her secret marriage to Lord Peterborough, and of the dramatic circumstances under which Lord Peterborough at last acknowledged her as his wife.

Again, there have been English singers who probably sang better than Lavinia Fenton—the original " Polly " of the *Beggars' Opera*. But she is one of the few vocalists who have had an English Duke for husband, besides which his Grace ran away with her ; and, most important point of all, the elopement was chronicled and commented on by Swift.

The life of a young lady who, born with great musical gifts, cultivates them in the most appropriate manner, and after gaining the favour of the public enjoys it tranquilly until, getting married to a gentleman in her own station, she retires and lives irreproachably to a good old age ; such a life recommends itself to the moralist but not to the biographer.

Of the great vocalists whose lives I have endeavoured to trace some from the humblest rank have become Queens of Song ; and one, at least, from a high social position returned to the stage in order to retrieve the fortunes of the Ambassador who had made her his wife.   Another, when her husband had been struck down in battle, hurried to the field ambulance where he lay wounded in order to nurse him.   A good many of my heroines, too, have got into trouble more or less dramatic in connection with marriage and even with divorce.

No prima donna has, except in the usual feminine way, committed a murder ; and only one, the unfor-

tunate Madame Huberti, or de Saint Huberti, was
ever murdered. Several, however, have caused
duels ; and Mdlle. de Maupin, to whom I have
accorded a brief notice, without making her the
subject of a separate chapter, was herself a
duellist.

Madame Huberti, moreover, apart from her tragic
end, was beloved by Napoleon. She, at least,
inspired him with sufficient admiration to make him
address to her some highly complimentary verses ;
and the life of this distinguished vocalist was full
of dramatic incidents.

In 1784 Sacchini's *Chimène*, adapted from *Il
Gran Cid*, an opera he had written for our King's
Theatre in 1773, was produced at the Académie of
Paris with great success, and with Madame Huberti
in the principal part. This vocalist was much
admired by Piccinni, who wrote some airs in the
cantabile style expressly for her, and said that
without her his opera of *Dido*, in which she played
the principal part, was " without Dido." M. Castil
Blaze tells us that she was the first true vocalist who
appeared at the Académie. Grimm declares that
she sang like Todi and acted like Clairon. Finally,
when Madame de Saint Huberti was performing at
Strasburg in 1787, a young officer of artillery,
named Napoleon Bonaparte, sent her these ingenious verses :—

Romains, qui vous vantez d'une illustre origine
Voyez d'où dépendait votre empire naissant ;
Didon n'eut pas de chaîne assez puissant
Pour arrêter la fuite où son amant s'obstine ;
Mais si l'autre Didon, ornement de ces lieux,
          Eût été reine de Carthage
Il eût, pour la servir, abandonné ces dieux,
Et votre beau pays serait encore sauvage.

After flying from Paris during the Reign of Terror Madame Huberti married the Count D'Entraigues, whom at great personal risks she had succeeded in liberating from prison; and she seemed now to have terminated her operatic career happily and honourably.

The Countess always wore the order of St. Michael, which had been given to her by the then unacknowledged Louis XVIII. in token of the services she had rendered to the Royalist party by saving from the revolutionists at once the Count D'Entraigues and the Count D'Entraigues' portfolio, which contained political papers of great importance. The Count afterwards entered the service of Russia, and was entrusted by the Government with several confidential missions. Hitherto he had been working in the interest of the Bourbons against Napoleon. But when the French Emperor and the Emperor Alexander formed an alliance after the battles of Eylau and Friedland he seems to have thought that his connection with Russia ought to terminate; and he was obliged to fly from Dresden in order to escape arrest at the hands of Napoleon's agents. Then he found means to obtain a copy of the secret articles in the treaty of Tilsit. So, at least, he said ; and he sold for a large sum of money to the English Government what he declared to be the articles in question ; though according to M. Thiers (*Histoire du Consulat et de l'Empire*) the document was false, and the money he received for it "*mal gagné.*" For his services to the English Government he is said to have received a pension; and he now established himself in England, where he appears to have had continual relations with the Foreign Office.

The French police heard how the Count D'Entraigues was occupied in England, and Fouché sent over two agents to watch him and, if possible, intercept his letters. These emissaries employed an Italian refugee to get acquainted with and bribe Lorenzo, the Count's servant ; who allowed his compatriot to read and even take copies of the despatches frequently entrusted to him by his master for conveyance to Mr. Canning. Lorenzo, moreover, gave the agent a number of the Count's letters to and from other persons.

One evening a letter was brought to M. D'Entraigues which obliged him to go early the next day from his house at Barnes to London. Lorenzo had observed the seal of the Foreign Office on the envelope, and saw, or fancied he saw, that his

treachery would soon be discovered.   In the morning
everything was ready for the journey, when he stabbed
his master, who fell to the ground mortally wounded.
The Countess was getting into the carriage.   To
prevent her charging him with her husband's death
the servant stabbed her also, and a few moments
afterwards, in confusion and despair, blew his own
brains out with a pistol which he in the first
instance appears to have intended for M. D'Entraigues.   This horrible affair occurred on the 22nd
of July, 1812.

I have been assured by an impresario who has
always been considered worthy of credit that there
exists and that he possesses a sort of operatic stud-
book compiled for the instruction and protection of
managers ; who, trusting implicitly in the representations made to them by singers in want of an engagement, might at times be deceived.   The directory
in question gives the exact age (obtained in many
cases at great labour and expense) of all the artists
before the public ; the date on which each of them
appeared for the first time on the stage ; the degree
of success obtained, and so on.   Among the in-
dications given by this valuable work is the name of
the professor answerable for each singer's style ;
though here the author of the operatic stud-book
goes, perhaps, into unnecessary details.

What chiefly concerns the public, and almost equally the manager, in regard to a singer is her talent as a result—not the means by which she acquired it.

If Mr. Irving were a tenor, half a dozen different singing-masters, each with his own particular system for forming, forcing, flattening, sharpening, or otherwise destroying the natural voice, would have contested in public the honour of having trained him. But nobody has yet heard who (if anyone) claims to have given him the power of arresting and holding, as much by appealing to its imagination as to its intelligence, the attention of an audience.

Still, though it may be questioned whether the art of acting can be taught, no such doubt can be entertained on the subject of singing — given a beautiful voice and some natural faculty for using it.

The art of singing is said by some professors to be dying out, and it is probably just now in a decline ; which may in a measure be accounted for by the declamatory character of a large proportion of modern operas. If audiences think more at present of the music of an opera than of the manner in which the music is sung, that fact is in itself not in the least to be regretted. But it ought not to be forgotten that many modern singers can scarcely be considered vocalists. Declamation, more or less dramatic, is to singing what mimetic action in a

ballet is to dancing. The two things are of the same
nature, but they are different in kind ; and as a mime
may be unable to dance, so it often happens as a
matter of fact that a declamatory artist is unable to
sing. In the training of a dramatic vocalist singing
and declamation should each have their part; and
as those walk best who have learned to dance, so to
excel in declamation it is necessary in the first place
to have studied singing. Naturally, too, the singing
of exercises should precede the singing of airs ; and
here one is reminded that the falling-off in the art of
vocalization may partly be accounted for by the
practice which certain teachers, or rather trainers,
pursue of giving their pupils operatic parts to learn
before instructing them in the most ordinary rudiments, the most essential principles.

The story of the old Italian singing-master who
kept a favourite pupil for years at scale passages,
intervals, and shakes, until at last, on the young
man's asking whether the day would ever come when
he might be allowed to attempt an air, he was told
that he might attempt anything with the fullest confidence, for that he was now the first singer in the
world :—this story is either untrue, or, if true, mis-
leading ; since, by the study of exercises alone, me-
chanical perfection is all that can be acquired. Intelligence, poetical feeling, dramatic expression, are
also necessary if the singer is not only to astonish the

ears, but also, and above all, to touch the hearts of his hearers. Still, the diminution in the number of good singers is due, in the first place, to abandonment or neglect of preliminary and fundamental studies; and it is startling to be told, on such unimpeachable authority as that of Signor Delle Sedie, in his " Estetica del Canto," that it is quite rare, "particularly with operatic artists," to find a voice " wisely conducted, using all sounds homogeneously, expressively, feelingly, and capable of modulating them according to the meaning of the words."

The origin of these faults is often to be found in an imperfect artistic education, or in an absolutely bad direction of the vocalist's studies. But causes of a more general kind must have been at work, when, as is too often the case, one hears love, hatred, jealousy, wrath, joy, and sorrow expressed with inflexions of voice almost uniform.

In most cases the eulogizer of bygone times is merely repeating a kind of blame and a form of praise which, from generation to generation, has been heard for centuries. But the singing-masters of the eighteenth century do not seem to have complained that the art of singing was dying out; and as a matter of fact there are, in the present day, fewer great singers, fewer singers capable of rousing an audience to enthusiasm than there were fifty or sixty years ago, when Pasta, Malibran, and Sontag were all before the public. In the year 1869, however, at a time when the art of singing was already said to have expired, Adelina Patti, Pauline Lucca, and Christine Nilsson were all singing together at the Royal Italian Opera—which did not look like decadence; and if since 1843, the fortunate period which saw the birth of this incomparable trio, nature has been somewhat niggardly in the matter of prime donne (as is sufficiently proved by the three ladies just named being still, after a quarter of a century's pre-eminence, the first vocalists of their time), that must be accounted for, not by any neglect of necessary studies on the part of operatic aspirants, but simply by a dearth of beautiful voices. The singing-master has his uses, no doubt, and everyone knows that, although singing comes by nature rather more than do reading and writing, yet study is indispensable for vocalists as for artists of every other description. The one great exception to this rule seems to have been Mario, who never took a lesson in singing except when Meyerbeer taught him the part of "Raymond" in *Robert le Diable.* Meyerbeer, it need scarcely be said, was not a singing-master; he had no infallible "method," like the singing-masters who begin by telling their pupils that all they have learnt before coming to them is absolutely useless, that their manner of producing the voice is altogether wrong, and so on.

The singers of the present day know more of
music if less of singing than those singers of the
past, who spent so much time in merely practising
exercises. The faults which Delle Sedie points out
in the stage singing of the present day are due to
defective intelligence, want of education, and absence
of artistic feeling; to shortcomings, that is to say,
on those very points where Mario excelled.

The fact that Patti, Lucca, Nilsson, and Albani
have, one after the other, been engaged year after
year at the Royal Italian Opera or at Her Majesty's
Theatre for leading soprano parts constitutes an excellent reason for devoting more space to them than
to other vocalists also of the highest merit who have
not been so often, or for so long a time, before the
London public. But why, it may be asked, should
Persiani not have a chapter to herself? Persiani who
shared (not quite equally) the honours of Her
Majesty's Theatre with Grisi, under the management
of Mr. Lumley, and of his predecessor, Mr. Laporte?
It was for her that Donizetti wrote the part of
" Lucia," which alone would stamp her as one of the
first—and not in time alone—of light sopranos.
Fifty or sixty years ago, before *Lucia* was written,
and before Meyerbeer had begun systematically to
compose in his grand operas one part for a light
soprano and one part for a " strong " soprano,

singers seem to have been classed by their dramatic rather than by their vocal qualities; and even now the " strong " soprano figures almost exclusively in serious opera, though the domain of the light soprano extends far beyond the regions of the comic, and includes a majority of the chief sentimental parts. Nevertheless, the distinction is now above all dependent on the voice. There are parts for singers with thin, flexible voices, and parts for singers with full, sonorous voices; and thus two distinct sets of qualities are cultivated which no one expects to find united in the same artist. In the present day we should no more expect to see a Persiani appear as " Semiramide " than we should have expected a Titiens to appear as " Amina; " while a Patti would seem to be as much out of place in the character of " Norma " as a Titiens would really have been out of place in that of " Rosina." Meyerbeer is known to have done more than any other composer to establish the now very appreciable difference between the light and heavy soprano, which in several of his operas, and notably in *Les Huguenots*, are in striking contrast. It would be difficult to say which of the two voices Meyerbeer himself preferred; for though in *L'Africane*, *Le Prophète*, and *Les Huguenots* the light soprano comes off second best, he has presented in *Dinorah* one of the most charming light soprano parts ever written.

Persiani, however, sang before the days of Meyerbeer, or rather before the days when Meyerbeer was
fairly naturalized in England; though it was to
Madame Persiani, and, above all, Signor Persiani,
her husband, that we owe the establishment of the
Royal Italian Opera, where Meyerbeer's works were,
for the first time in England, played in something
like their integrity. Or, it is they, as the case may
otherwise be put, who are responsible for having
destroyed the monopoly virtually enjoyed until the
year 1846 by Her Majesty's Theatre; a monopoly
such as may be beneficial to art, however injurious to
commerce.

For about a dozen years Persiani was engaged at
Her Majesty's Theatre simultaneously with Grisi,
and, like her, shared the successes of Rubini, Tamburini, and Lablache. Born in 1812, at Rome, she
was the daughter of Tacchinardi, a famous tenor;
and she made her *début* a few years later than
Giulia Grisi. After several not very successful
appearances in operas of doubtful value, some of
them the composition of Signor Persiani, whom she
married at an early age, she made a most favourable
impression in the *Gazza Ladra*, of Rossini; the
Pirata, of Bellini; and the *Elisir d'Amore*, of Donizetti. After fulfilling an engagement at La Scala
she was invited to Naples, and there, at the San
Carlo Theatre, created the part of "Lucia" in

what is generally looked upon as Donizetti's master-piece. So it was considered by Rossini at the time of its production, 1835 ; and the composer can scarcely be said to have surpassed it in any of his later works. In the first performances of *Lucia di Lammermoor* Persiani as " Lucia " was associated with Duprez as " Edgardo."

It was as " Lucia " that she made her first appearance at the Théâtre des Italiens of Paris ; and from Paris she soon passed to London. Here, at the King's Theatre, she distinguished herself in a number of parts of the light soprano type, with " Lucia," and afterwards " Linda," prominent among them. As " Adina " in *L'Elisir d'Amore* was also one of her happiest impersonations, she may be said to have been intimately connected with some of the greatest successes of Donizetti ; though neither her talent nor the character of her voice rendered her suitable for so emphatically dramatic a part as that of " Lucrezia Borgia."

Madame Persiani's genius was especially for vocalization, and though there was pathos in her acting it was pathos of the elegiac, not of the tragic kind. It was as " Amina " in *La Sonnambula* that Persiani made her first appearance in London ; the part in which Pasta, for whom it was written, and Malibran, who in London made it her most successful impersonation, so often sang ; the part in which years afterwards so many *débutantes* were still to appear, with Patti, Albani, and Gerster among them. Persiani was a singer who pleased, charmed, and even delighted her hearers without greatly impressing them—certainly without electrifying them by any of those bursts of passion for which Grisi was famous. Mr. Chorley, never willing to accord full praise, says in regard to Persiani's singing that "every conceivable passage was finished by her to perfection, the shake, perhaps, excepted, which might be thought indistinct and thin." On the other hand, her execution, according to the same authority, was "remarkable for velocity, poignant, clear, audacious."

Madame Persiani died near Paris in 1867, when she had already for something like twenty years been lost sight of by the public. Her career was, indeed, a very short one for so well-trained, so accomplished a vocalist. So far as England is concerned she passed out of sight after the opening season (1847) of the Royal Italian Opera, where she was replaced by Madame Castellan; a very charming singer, though less perfect by a good deal than Madame Persiani. Her marriage with Signor Persiani, musical conductor and composer, cannot be said to have proved beneficial to her interests, since it was owing to the cabal which he started in 1846 against Mr. Lumley that she soon afterwards found herself excluded even from the theatre where he had apparently hoped that she would reign supreme.

A word here as to Signor Persiani himself, who began life as an orchestral conductor, and who was known, moreover, as a composer of several operas.

Next to the principal singers the most important personage at an opera-house is, undoubtedly, the conductor. Indeed, the " conductor of the orchestra," as he is sometimes called, is often, in an artistic point of view, conductor of the entire establishment. To hold such a position he should be an administrator as well as an artist, nor will it lessen his utility if he is at the same time an excellent stage-manager. He need not be a composer in the creative sense of the word. But in a country where operas in five acts are simply not tolerated he must know how to shorten a work without spoiling it. He must be able to " cut " it without wasting too much of the master's blood, to join together pieces on which he has operated in such a manner that no scar shall be visible. Thirty or forty years ago, when England was just emerging from musical barbarism, an operatic conductor was called " conductor and composer of the music; " a title which he retained long after his functions as composer had happily come to an end. Nothing at that time was sacred to this musical sapper, who

introduced himself where one would have least
expected to find him ; digging holes and inserting
his own diabolical contrivances into every work he
touched. Rossini's *Cenerentola,* Auber's *Muette
de Portici,* the same composer's *Diamants de la
Couronne,* may be mentioned among the operas
which chiefly suffered at the hands of these ruthless
" conductors and composers of the music," who,
reversing the crime of the plagiarist, attributed
their own weak inventions to men incapable of
such things.

The operatic conductor is no longer expected to
write new overtures to the works brought out under
his superintendence, nor to supply them with
" taking " tunes, nor to meddle with them in any
way except now and then when the limits of
English endurance require that they should be
shortened. No conductor has yet discovered the
art of curtailing a five-act masterpiece so as to
satisfy at once the critical and uncritical portions of
the public. " Leave out whole musical pieces if you
must do so, but don't mutilate the pieces you
retain," is the advice that would be given on this
head by musicians and true amateurs. But the
uncritical portion of the public, who read the libretto
instead of listening to the music, want to follow the
story ; and in their interest the conductor, instigated
or at least not discouraged by the manager, makes

havoc with the music in order that the too fortunate
" words " may in some measure be spared.

The operatic conductor is consulted as to what
new singers shall be engaged, what new operas
produced ; while the composition of the orchestra is
left absolutely to him. His interests, identical in
the long run with those of the manager, seem often
opposed to them, and managers have been heard to
say that their conductors " wished to ruin them."
This must have been a mistake. The conductor
never wishes to ruin the manager, which in many
cases would mean the ruin of the conductor himself.
But one can understand his subordinating economic
to purely artistic considerations ; for which reason,
as before remarked, the conductor should be something of an administrator, and should have clear
notions as to what is possible and what impossible
in the way of expenditure.

A really able conductor is the manager's friend,
though the manager may be excused for not thinking
so when the conductor, in his passion for a perfect
orchestra, proposes an outlay which the theatre
cannot afford. A really able conductor is also
the singer's best friend. But the singer is not
always aware of it, and will complain bitterly if
(for example) the conductor will not allow the time
in this passage to be unduly dragged, or in that one
unduly hastened. The singer and the orchestra

should work harmoniously together, neither endeavouring to shine at the other's expense. But it does certainly seem at times as though a fight were going on between the two, the orchestra exclaiming with its powerful voice : " You shall *not* be heard," the singer replying with a shriek : " I *will* be heard, whatever you may do to the contrary."

The public seems always well disposed towards the conductor. The nature, and above all, the extent of his functions are not, perhaps, generally understood. But it is clear from the elevated position assigned to him, and from the control he visibly exercises over the musicians, that he is a personage of no small importance ; and a brilliant orchestral performance always secures for him (as in justice it should) a large amount of applause. Next to a beautiful voice nothing is so effective as a fine band. The sweetness of the one, the sonority of the other, can be appreciated by everyone, and are alike irresistible.

Up to the year 1846 Her Majesty's Theatre had been so long recognized as the home of Italian Opera that Mr. Lumley, the impresario of the period, was supposed to possess a monopoly of the article, and an exclusive right to engage Italian artists in this country. His exceptional position, filled for many years with considerable ability, made him, unfortunately for himself, heed-

less of opposition. In or about the year given
above he quarrelled with Signor Persiani, husband
of the famous prima donna, through refusing to
produce an opera of his composition. To that
quarrel, and a reserved, autocratic bearing towards
his artists, may be traced all the rivalry against
which Mr. Lumley had subsequently to contend.

Persiani, if not a wealthy man, contrived to
make his friends believe that he had unlimited
capital at his command. He was on intimate terms
with all the singers under engagement to Mr.
Lumley, and succeeded in inducing the most attractive among them, with one exception, to leave the
manager on the termination of their contracts. The
exception was Lablache, who refused to forsake Her
Majesty's Theatre ; the great basso being probably
less exacting than his more sensitive colleagues, and
indifferent to the "autocratic" bearing of the impresario.

The disaffection of the rest is really not a matter
for surprise, considering the sort of antagonism
which almost invariably exists between a successful
manager and those under his control. It seems to
be inseparable from the relations between them. "I
have heard," writes Mr. Willert Beale on this
subject, " the most popular impresario reviled at
times as a *brigand en gants blancs*, and otherwise
abused behind his back, for the simplest act of

policy in the management of his theatre. Mr. Lumley did not care to soothe this feeling; he paid court to his subscribers but socially neglected his artists, and the moment came when the latter rebelled and renounced allegiance to him.

"Having gradually formed a powerful operatic company in Paris, Persiani arrived in London with a partner named Galletti, and with a still more important travelling companion in the shape of a letter of credit upon Rothschild for the sum of £35,000. In the course of time the partner proved to be a man of straw, while the letter of credit and guarantee was not available, having been retired when most urgently required.

"Persiani and Galletti took Covent Garden Theatre on lease, and having done so found that they were unequal to the task of managing the undertaking they intended to establish. They looked about for a representative, and found one in my father, the founder of the firm of Cramer and Co., and I may say, with all truth, that they were lucky in doing so, although to the object of their choice the result was most unexpected. My father was an enthusiastic pioneer in the cause of music. He was immensely popular with all branches of the musical profession in London and the provinces, and especially well-known for being concerned in the principal musical undertakings throughout the kingdom. He was, moreover, a practical musician, and acknowledged to be a first-rate violoncellist, with a pure, sympathetic tone and great command of the bow. As a publisher he fostered and encouraged talent wherever he could meet with it. In the early days of their career he substantially assisted Balfe, Benedict, Loder, Wallace, Macfarren, Thalberg, and others innumerable, by publishing and aiding with his money and influence the public performance of their compositions. He was the first to issue an edition of Beethoven's works in England.

" The subscriptions for the first season from the librarians and the public amounted to little short of £25,000. The rehearsals of *Semiramide* took place before the scaffolding was removed and while the workmen were still employed in completing the decorations of the house. I was on the stage when Alboni came to rehearsal for the first time. She had not been heard by anyone in the theatre, and did not display the full power of her voice. But her singing *sotto voce* produced a sensation; the band and chorus applauded her involuntarily. The recitative ' Eccomi alfin in Babylonia' made a deep impression upon Grisi, who listened to the new contralto with evident astonishment. After going through the duet ' Giorno d'Orrore,' Donna Guilia resumed her seat, near which I was standing. 'What a glorious voice, and what singing!' she exclaimed, in excitement. The enthusiasm became general, and the unexpected revelation of a star of the first magnitude raised the hopes of all concerned in the prospects of the Royal Italian Opera. And hope required some such stimulant, for ominous clouds were already gathering in the horizon.

"The performance of *Semiramide* on the 6th April, 1847, was a brilliant commencement of the Royal Italian Opera from an artistic point of view. The *éclat* of the enterprise then started was further enhanced by the frustration of three different attempts to set fire to the theatre during the progress of the alterations. The origin of the three conflagrations, which were luckily extinguished, was never discovered, but strong evidence remained of their being the work of an incendiary. The reconstruction and decoration of the house created a favourable impression; the *salle* was thought to present a nobler appearance than that of Her Majesty's Theatre; the *foyers* and corridors were luxurious and spacious, and were generally approved by the subscribers. The *ensemble* of such a band and chorus as had been brought together was a novelty upon the lyric stage in the early days of the Royal Italian Opera; and this, together with the *début* of Alboni, of whose surprising vocal powers not a word in anticipation had been said, the genius of Grisi, then in its zenith, the splendour of the *mise en scène,* and the completeness of the representation as a whole, excited the enthusiasm of partisans to the highest pitch, and gave an effect to the performance of *Semiramide* on the date referred to which, according to outward appearances, guaranteed the success of the new undertaking beyond all doubt. But there was trouble behind the scenes. Persiani had taken fright. He renewed a stipulated sum of £5,000 twice, and then made excuses to delay further payment, being alarmed at the cost of rebuilding, the terrific salaries he had undertaken to pay when forming his operatic company, and the current expenses.

"The letter of credit upon Rothschild for £35,000, which had not been discounted, vanished; Galletti, the so-called partner, had no means."

It is not every great singer who, like Madame Grisi, Madame Patti, and a few others, enjoys a long career; and Madame Alboni, one of the greatest singers who ever lived, was before the public for only a few years. In England she was first heard in 1847, when, unheralded by praise or by mention of any kind, she came out at the Royal Italian Opera; her perfect vocalization, both as regards expression and execution, forming one of the principal attractions in the opening performance when *Semiramide* was played with Grisi in the part of the wicked heroine, with Tamburini as " Assur," and Alboni as " Arsace." It would be difficult to name any first appearance on the operatic stage—except only that of Madame Patti, made under like circumstances —which so completely took the audience by surprise and, surprising them, filled them at the same time with delight. Like Adelina Patti, Marietta Alboni was, at least to the audience, absolutely unknown; and no one among the public knew whether she was a singer of the first or of the fourth class until by her delivery of the first few words of "Arsace's " opening recitative she at once awakened the enthusiasm of the whole house. In the course of that first memorable season, Alboni, with her rich, full voice, her absolutely just intonation, her versatility and her *verve,* made a striking success in every part she undertook; especially in those of " Arsace," of " Maffeo Orsini " in *Lucrezia Borgia,* and of " Betly " in Donizetti's pretty rustic opera, based on the same subject as the *Châlet* of Adolphe Adam.

It has already been mentioned, on the authority of Mr. Willert Beale, that at one of the last rehearsals of *Semiramide,* with which the newly-organized Royal Italian Opera was to begin its career, Grisi on hearing the new " Arsace " uttered a cry of admiration. The beauty of the singer's voice filled her with astonishment. She must have wondered also whence could have come the possessor of such a voice which she now heard for the first time. The establishment of the Royal Italian Opera was followed by an immediate collapse; but it did not fall until the first season had been duly brought to its appointed end; and before the time for the following season had arrived it was set up again. Meanwhile, however, Alboni had gone; and she was now to visit Paris, and next to reappear in London, not, however, at the Royal Italian Opera, but at Her Majesty's Theatre. Then, after a public life of not more than eight or nine years, the Countess Pepoli, as she had now become, retired, and was never again heard of by the musical world except when, at long intervals and generally for some charitable purpose, she consented to appear at some concert of a special kind.

During her engagement at the Grand Opera or Académie Royale of Paris she appeared as the heroine of *La Corbeille d'Oranges*, a work written specially for her by Auber, but not in Auber's best nor even in his prettiest style. Having heard this opera on the occasion of its first performance more than thirty years ago, all I can now remember of it, and all that impressed me in it at the time, is one moderately graceful and melodious, but neither very refined nor very original, air in six-eight time for the leading vocalist.

Appearing without any preliminary announcement, Madame Alboni disappeared without any formal farewell. In no country where, so far as that country was concerned, she sang for the last time were her admirers allowed to realize the fact that they were never to hear her again. No singer had a finer sense of art, with which she combined an entire absence of vanity and of that greediness for money which in the present day renders a well-organized operatic enterprise all but impossible. On her retirement she married Count Pepoli.

Of the generosity of Madame Alboni's disposition striking evidence was given when, soon after Rossini's death, it was, under peculiar circumstances, suggested to her by Maurice Strakosch that she should sing the important contralto part in the lamented composer's *Petite Messe Solennelle*, written for piano, harmonium, four soloists, and a chorus of sixteen voices. Vexed at the coldness with which *Guillaume Tell* had been received, not by the public but by the manager to whom the fortunes of the Paris Opera-house were at that time entrusted, Rossini (according to Strakosch) resolved that " no new work from his pen should be brought out during his life-time." Yet the Stabat Mator was produced, and after a private performance of the Mass, at which Alboni was present, the great Italian composer said, that if after his death the work was executed in public he hoped she would undertake the contralto part which he had in a certain sense written for her. When, not long after Rossini's death, Maurice Strakosch arranged with Madame Rossini to give public performances of the Mass, he was very anxious that the contralto part should be sung by Alboni, to whose voice it was particularly suited. But the Countess Pepoli assured him that she had resolved to sing no more in public. In the course of conversation, however, she mentioned to Strakosch that a favourite niece who had for some time been engaged could not marry for want of a dowry.

" How much do you wish to give her ? " asked the impresario ; and finding that the sum thought necessary was one hundred thousand francs, and that Alboni wished to have it in three months, he promised to guarantee her that sum within the time specified if she would only sing the contralto part in Rossini's Mass. The Mass was performed four times at the Italian Theatre of Paris during the first month, and sixty times during the two following months in various parts of France, Belgium, and Holland ; and the hundred thousand francs were paid by Strakosch to Madame Alboni and by Madame Alboni settled as dowry on her niece.

Madame Alboni's associates on the tour were Mdlle. Marie Battu (who created the second soprano part in Meyerbeer's *Africaine*) ; Mr. Tom Hohler, one of our most successful tenors, who, after retiring from the stage, married the Duchess of Newcastle ; and Signor Agnesi—an excellent cast.

Alboni was born in 1824, at Cesena, in the Romagna, and she made her first appearance at the Scala of Milan in 1843, as " Maffeo Orsini: " a part which she afterwards sung with the greatest success at the Royal Italian Opera, and subsequently at Her Majesty's Theatre.

Sophie Cruvelli (Cruwel by her real name) will be remembered as one of the three or four singers of German origin who, like Schroeder-Devrient and Sontag—the first so to distinguish herself—obtained a European reputation. Born in Westphalia in 1826, she began her career boldly, as befitted a vocalist of high ambition, by singing for the first time in Italy. Here she obtained her earliest successes in the operas of Verdi, with whom one associates her much as Madame Persiani is associated with Donizetti, though in a less degree than that in which Madame Colbran is associated with the great Italian successes, from *Otello* to *Semiramide,* of Rossini. For many years Sophie Cruvelli's greatest part was that of " Elvira " in *Ernani;* but the only part in an opera by Verdi which she " created" was that of " Hélène " in *Les Vépres Siciliennes,* when she was on the point of leaving the stage. One of her grandest imperso-nations was that of " Valentine " in *Les Huguenots;*

though grander still was her "Fidelio," which she played in London with the greatest possible success. Meyerbeer, so long in search for a suitable representative of "Selika" in *L'Africaine*, found at last in Mdlle. Cruvelli all that he required. But it was too late. She was about to retire, and *L'Africaine* was not brought out until after his death; when the part, which, at a later period, was to be undertaken with so much success by Madame Pauline Lucca, was assigned to Madame Saxe—or Madame Sasse, as she was compelled to describe herself when, on the complaint of M. Adolphe Sax, inventor of the saxhorn, she was ordered to resume her true name.

Mdlle. Maria Piccolomini was one of the singers on whom Mr. Lumley relied to retrieve himself after the departure of Jenny Lind, and when the success of the Royal Italian Opera had deprived him of much patronage. Inheritress of an historic name, which in England was little known except to readers of Schiller, and which was generally mispronounced, she came from Siena, where she was born in 1834. With a charming face and rather a plump figure, more remarkable for winning ways than for commanding talent, Piccolomini made her first appearance at the Pergola of Florence in the somewhat inappropriate part of "Lucrezia Borgia." It has

been pointed out, however, again and again in these
volumes that the distinction now so marked between
light soprano and dramatic soprano is modern, not
to say recent. "Norma" was one of Jenny Lind's
favourite parts. The graceful Bosio appeared at
St. Petersburg as "Semiramide;" and probably at
Florence in 1852 no one saw anything strange in
the character of "Lucrezia" being assigned to a
pretty, piquant little soubrette, with a strong vein
of sentiment in her, and with enough vivacity and
verve for anything.

When Mdlle. Piccolomini made her *début* at
Florence the opera in which she was to achieve her
greatest success had not been composed, or, at
least, had not yet been produced. In 1852 Verdi
saw the *Dame aux Camélias* of the younger Dumas
at Paris, and resolved to set it to music. His
librettist, Piave, struck out the comedy scenes
and all that marked too characteristically the
ignoble society in the midst of which Marguerite
Gautier passed her existence; and, retaining all the
dramatic scenes and the pathetic scene with which
the piece terminates, arranged the whole for musical
setting. Early in 1853 the work was ready for
production, and it was brought out at the Fenice of
Venice March the 6th in that year.

The opera failed; partly because the public could
not take kindly to a work based on a modern novel,

chiefly of manners, and presenting scenes of a kind never treated in music before. The piece was played at the first representation in the dress of the present day; which has been proved in several instances, when the costumes are those of the drawing-room and of town life generally, to be impossible on the operatic stage. *Don Pasquale* for many years after its first production, in 1843, was played with the three male characters in the ordinary frock-coats and dress-coats of modern European life. But the realism of every-day existence is not adapted for musical setting, and after a few years it was found absolutely necessary to place the action of *Don Pasquale* in a past age. *La Traviata* had to be treated in similar fashion; and Auber's *Domino Noir* is now the only opera in which the male characters appear in the dull, prosaic attire of our own time.

But the main reason, according to Verdi himself, why *La Traviata* failed at Venice was the imperfect manner in which it was executed. The night after the first performance he wrote to a friend saying that his opera had met with no success.

" Whose fault was it," he went on to ask, " mine or the singers ?   Time will show."

Time has indeed shown that *La Traviata* is one of the brightest, and, in a dramatic point of view, one of the best of Verdi's operas.   The subject is not a

pleasant one, and there is still an impression among
many persons that the frivolity of which the story
is largely made up is reproduced in the music.
This, however, is not the case. Piave, in his well-
constructed libretto, confines himself to the really
striking situations; and Verdi's treatment of the
finale to the third act (which contains one of the
most eloquent phrases he ever wrote), and of the
last act, from beginning to end, is quite masterly.

One quite sufficient reason why *La Traviata* did
not succeed on the occasion of its first representation was that the part of the unhappy heroine was
taken by a "light soprano," whose lightness lay
wholly in her voice, and whose figure was of massive
proportions. Accordingly, when she exclaimed that
she was wasting away, that she had not many hours
to live, and so on, the audience, unable to restrain
their mirth, burst into roars of laughter.

When, however, the work was sung with a vocalist
refined in appearance as well as in style for the
representative of "Violetta" it obtained, as Verdi
had foreseen, the greatest success; and the first
prima donna who triumphed in the part was Piccolomini. It was in the Carignan Theatre of Turin, in
1855, that she appeared as "Violetta" for the first
time; and the year afterwards she undertook the
part in London with the effect of filling Her
Majesty's Theatre to overflowing at each successive

performance. Apart from its musical success, the opera had a *succès de scandale;* for the *Times* published day after day long letters, in which the work was now attacked, now defended. It was generally admitted that the opera was not one of those to which a girl could take her mother. At the same time a great deal of nonsense was written about a work which was not likely to affect anyone, in a moral point of view, either favourably or unfavourably. If *La Traviata* exercises no corrupting influence, neither can it be said to teach a salutary lesson. Highwaymen, said Dr. Johnson, would not believe that they could rob with impunity, because in the *Beggar's Opera* they saw " Macheath " forgiven; and we may be sure that no " Traviata " in real life will forsake the errors of her ways from seeing "Violetta" perish of consumption.

Mdlle. Piccolomini used to remind the audience that "Violetta" was wasting away from phthisis by coughing at intervals throughout the piece; an objectionable touch of realism which Bosio, when soon afterwards she undertook the part, first at St. Petersburg and afterwards at the Royal Italian Opera, had the good taste not to reproduce.

Mdlle. Piccolomini appeared as the heroine of Verdi's " Luisa Miller," and in several other parts, including that of "Adina" in the *Elixir of Love.*

As " Adina " she was altogether charming; simple,
without the least affectation, and engaging, as such
a heroine should be.

Mr. Henry Morley, who gives a very interesting
account of Mdlle. Piccolomini in his " Recollections
of an old Play-goer," speaks of "Adina" as one of
her best parts.   This it certainly was, though it is
by her " Violetta" (which, with all its faults, was
a very touching and dramatic impersonation) that
she will be chiefly remembered.

Mdlle. Piccolomini, when she had been only a few
years on the stage, married the Marquis Gaetani
and retired.   She did not suffer from that passion
for money by which so many prime donne of the
present day are devoured; and when, in 1863,
she heard that a series of performances were to
be given at Her Majesty's Theatre for the benefit
of her old manager she came to England expressly
to give her services.

Ilma de Murska, unrivalled in certain romantic
and fantastic characters, such as " Astrafiammenta " in the *Magic Flute,* and " Dinorah " in the
opera of that name, and who was characteristically
successful in the mad scene of " Lucia," and
as " Senta " in the *Flying Dutchman,* is a
native of Croatia, and she was born in the great
vocalists' year of 1843 ; a year which must surely

be memorable in astronomical records from the
visit of some comet, or by some conjunction of
planets specially favourable to the production of
musical stars.   Adelina Patti, Christine Nilsson, and
Pauline Lucca were all born in this *annus mirabilis.*
So, too, according to all available documentary
evidence on the subject, was Ilma de Murska;
though by some accounts, including her own, she is
several years younger, while her enemies (and who
in the world of music, or in any world, is without
them ?) say she is some years older.   Ilma de Murska
is in any case an admirable singer, singing quite well
enough to have been born in the year 1843.

It is absolutely certain that this gifted and
accomplished vocalist, with a powerful individuality
of her own, after studying at Vienna and at Paris,
under Signor Marchesi, sang for the first time at
the Pergola of Florence in 1862, when, according
to the 1843 theory, she would have been 19 : a fair
age for a *débutante.*   She afterwards sang at Pesth,
Vienna, Berlin, and Hamburg, until in 1865 she
accepted an engagement at Her Majesty's Theatre
where she made her first appearance as " Lucia."
Plenty of admirable " Lucias " had already been
heard in London.   But Ilma de Murska surprised
everyone by the originality of her performance in
the scene of " Lucia's " madness ; and as she also
sang the brilliant music of the part in all possible

perfection her success was naturally very great. Her impersonation of " Lucia" was one of the sensations of the 1865 opera season ; and she renewed the marked impression which she had made in the character of " Lucia " by her singing in the part of " Astrafiammenta," and by her singing and acting conjointly in that of " Dinorah." Nothing more quaint, more fantastic, and at the same time more charming than Ilma de Murska's " Dinorah " has ever been seen on the operatic stage. In " Linda" and all the light soprano parts of the operatic repertory she was admirable. But a just idea of the special character of her talent can be formed from what has just been said as to her peculiar success in dealing with the fantastic.

Ilma de Murska sang the most difficult passages of ornamentation with unerring certainty ; and she possessed such a memory, combined with such a dislike for the worry of rehearsals, that she would frequently learn her part by simply reading it over while she was lying in bed.

There is much to console those who have bad memories in a paper recently communicated by M. Dulauney to the Société de Biologie of Paris. M. Dulauney has made a study of memory and its phenomena as observed among superior and inferior races, the educated and the uneducated, the old and the young. The force of memory, if

M. Dulauney's conclusions on the subject can be accepted, is differently exhibited among women and among men; and there is a summer memory as well as a winter memory, a memory of the morning and a memory of the evening. M. Dulauney's essay would have possessed more value if he had begun by telling us what he means by Memory; for, as a matter of fact, men and women in civilized society have often a good memory in connection with subjects which interest them, and a bad memory, or no memory at all, in connection with others. Rubinstein and Bülow, for instance, will play a dozen pianoforte pieces in succession without notes, and Mr. Brandram will recite an entire play of Shakespeare's without book. But Mr. Brandram may possibly lack musical memory altogether, and there is no reason for believing that either Bülow or Rubinstein possesses any special faculty in the way of remembering words.

However Mdlle. de Murska's exceptional memory may be accounted for, it in any case belonged to her; and she remembered her parts, not, like many untaught singers, from the sound of the tones, but from the aspect of the notes.

When Mdlle. de Murska visited Paris she made a decided impression, and on the whole a favourable one, though her striking merits did not pass absolutely unquestioned. "Lucia," own sister to "Linda," was her great part in Paris, and it was no slight proof of talent to be able to succeed in a *rôle* which the Parisians had taught themselves to believe could only be adequately filled by Mdme. Adelina Patti. Mdlle. de Murska never ceases to hold the attention of her audience. She is full of life, and every one of her gestures, and even glances, is significant. Sometimes, no doubt, she exaggerates, now in one direction, now in another; but she is never cold and never leaves the public unmoved. She even gives animation to "Marguerite de Valois," who, in the hands of most sopranos, is a mere singing automaton; while in the character of "Linda" she is full of vivacity in the brilliant scena of the first act and full of feeling in the touching and tragic scenes of Acts II. and III. Her delivery of the cavatina known (from the title of the quick movement) as " O luce di questa anima " is sparkling even to the point of effervescence.

The originality which distinguished Ilma de Murska on the stage was occasionally shown by her in private life. She turned up in the most unexpected places, and when she first visited London she gave a ball, which, beginning after the same night's performance, was (according to the invitations, one of which I had the honour of receiving) to be carried on until an advanced hour next morning, and then followed by a picnic in Kew Gardens. An early visitor to Kew Gardens on the morning in question is prepared to certify that at the appointed hour no signs of the promised picnic were to be seen.

Mdlle. de Murska has probably been married more than once. During a visit to Australia she became the wife of a violinist who soon after the marriage died. Unhappily for her no settlements had been made, and half her property passed away to her husband's relations.

One of the most Italian, by voice and style, of all the singers that of late years have appeared at our Italian Opera-houses is Madame Trebelli, who, nevertheless, is French by birth. She began her musical studies as a pianist under a German professor, then joined the singing classes of M. Wartel, and in 1859 made her first appearance on the operatic stage at Madrid. After fulfilling a two years' engagement in the Spanish capital, where, by her singing, her acting, and her beauty, she achieved the most brilliant success, Mdlle. Gillebert, or "Trebelli," as she now called herself, returned to Paris, where, in April, 1861, she appeared at the Théâtre des Italiens as "Rosina" in *Il Barbiere*, one of her finest impersonations. It seems strange in the present day that the part of "Rosina" should be assigned to a contralto, though, as a matter of fact, it was written for the contralto voice.

Engaged on the conclusion of her season at the Théâtre des Italiens by Signor Merelli, the well-known impresario, Mdlle. Trebelli made under his direction an artistic tour which carried her through the principal musical cities of North Germany, including Cologne, Berlin (where her singing provoked rapturous enthusiasm) and Hamburg. She again visited Paris and accepted an engagement at the Italian Theatre; the parts now assigned to her being those of the "Countess" (*Marriage of Figaro*); "Azucena" (*Il Trovatore*); "Amalia" (*Un Ballo in Maschera*); and "Maffeo Orsini" (*Lucrezia Borgia*). Brussels, Copenhagen, Leipsic, and Baden were in turn visited by the popular artist, whose reputation had now become European. Mdlle. Trebelli was also to renew her triumphs in Spain, and so successful was she in London that when once our public had heard her it refused to accept any other contralto as "Urbano," as "Nancy," or, above all, as "Maffeo Orsini." Adopted by English audiences as a vocalist with whose talent and charm they could not dispense, Mdlle. Trebelli on her side adopted England as her place of abode; and for years past she has lived among us.

Married more than twenty years ago to Signor

Bettini, Madame Trebelli sang for some years under the name of Trebelli-Bettini. In due time, however, the usual separation took place, the custody of the only child being adjudged to the mother. The child in question is already known as one of the most brilliant light sopranos of the day. Mdlle. Antoinette Trebelli, endowed by nature with a fresh flexible voice of much brightness and of constantly increasing power, has had the advantage of being directed in her studies by one of the most perfect vocalists of our time; and those who have heard mother and daughter singing together, as happened on the occasion of Mdlle. Antoinette Trebelli's *début* at St. James's Hall, may well hesitate as to which is most to be admired.

Whence, it is often asked, comes the name of Trebelli, so musical, so sonorous, and so significant? for "Trebelli" means "very beautiful," if we derive the word from the French; "thrice beautiful" if we trace it to the Italian.

There was once a learned jurisconsult named Trebellius. But he had nothing whatever to do with music, and why should Madame Trebelli have gone to him for a name?

Look, however, at the word Gillebert; consider it well, and it will be seen that "Gillebert" spelt backwards makes "Trebellig." Strike out the "g" and you have the charming contralto's operatic name.

Minnie Hauck, seemingly of German parentage, though she herself is American-English—cosmopolitan, in fact—sings with equal ease and success in English, Italian, French, German, and Hungarian. She was born at New York, November 16th, 1852, and came out in operatic parts when she was but thirteen. Then she retired for a time, but meanwhile studied assiduously under Signor Errani. After further successes in her native land she crossed the Atlantic, and before many years had made the tour of Europe. Beginning her European career at Vienna, she next came to London, and in October, 1868, made her first appearance at the Royal Italian Opera in the character of "Amina." The youthful Minnie was, at this time, singularly artless; and in the chamber scene where "Amina" lies down in bed she so gave herself up to the situation that she fell fast asleep. Fortunately the chorus of villagers was given in sufficiently loud tones to awaken in due time this by no means genuine somnambulist.

On another occasion, when she was rehearsing the part of "Violetta," she picked up and pocketed the bank-notes which the indignant "Alfredo" had cast at her feet. "What else," she thought, "would a woman of 'Violetta's' character be likely to do?"

Minnie Hauck is one of the few eminent vocalists who have made a first appearance in London during an autumn or winter season. Early in the century the fashionable season—the season of Court recep-

tions, balls, operas, concerts, and entertainments of
all kinds—took place during what may well be
considered the winter months, or at least the
months of winter and spring—from the beginning
of January to the beginning of May. It began
and ended just three months sooner than the
season of our own time, which lasts, as a rule, from
the beginning of April to the middle of July. Why
the London season has gradually, like the London
dinner-hour, got later and later, until what a
century ago was a winter season has become a
summer one, even as the dinner of a hundred years
ago has become very like a supper, it would be hard
to say. In both cases some natural law is no doubt at
work; but it is as inscrutable as the law which
in all the great European capitals determines a
constant movement among the richer and more
luxurious of the inhabitants towards the west.
This westward tendency on the part of the fashionable classes of Europe has been accounted for
in connection with the east wind, which, blowing from the Central Asian steppes, vexes the
people of Moscow, as, blowing from Bethnal Green,
and bringing with it clouds of dust, it irritates the
denizens of London.

It is certain, in any case, that London lies more
to the west, dines later by two or three hours, and
keeps its season later by three or four months than

it did at the beginning of the century. But as late dinners render lunches indispensable, so summer seasons seem at last to have forced people to get up a sort of imitation season in the winter; and a very good season in its way a winter season may be. Our winter evenings are long enough, our winter afternoons dark enough, to make it very desirable that something, and even a good deal, should be done in the way of public and private entertainments to dispel the prevailing gloom—that gloom which, as Bossuet declared in his famous denunciation of theatres, "forms the very substance of human life," and which, according to his view, cannot be chased away by stage representations, but only by meditation and prayer. A little harmless gaiety may also at times be efficacious.

Entertainment givers of all kinds seem, in any case, to be coming to the conclusion that the gloomy winter is a favourable period for their operations, and directors have discovered that people will listen to music in winter quite as readily as in summer.

But the question of the time of year at which opera singers should be heard must not take away our attention from the singers themselves. Of Minnie Hauck, however, there is little more to say, beyond the fact that she has sung in many countries, in many languages, and in many parts with one and the same success. Dutch is, at present, beyond her; but she gained much applause by introducing, when she was last in Holland, a few Dutch phrases into her part. Given the conditions of the performance in which Dutch and Italian were alternately employed, Mdlle. Hauck's harmless pleasantry was justifiable.

Mdlle. Hauck started in the autumn of last year to fulfil an engagement at St. Petersburg; and there is now no important country and no great capital in which she has not sung.

At Berlin some ten years ago she created the part of " Katherine " in the opera founded on the *Taming of the Shrew* by Goetz, whose fame as a writer of dramatic music rests on this work as that of Bizet rests on *Carmen*. Both these composers, each of whom might have been expected in his own country to found a new school of opera, neither so heavy as that of our laborious composers nor so light as that of our frivolous ones, died at an early age. Each of them left a masterpiece, and each of these masterpieces was introduced to the London public by Minnie Hauck.

It cannot, however, be said that Goetz's *Taming of the Shrew* has left in England or elsewhere any such impression as has been made by *Carmen*. Goetz's too elaborate recitatives, and the disproportionate space occupied by them, may have had

something to do with its failure to obtain popularity
in any wide sense of the word. *Carmen,* on the
other hand, is so full of movement, of melody,
of delicate harmonies and ingenious points of
orchestration, it is so dramatic, moreover, and
so picturesque that from the very first a long
life and a happy one might safely have been predicted for it. The score contains but little music
of the *cantabile* kind; though it included in its
original form two complete airs for " Carmen "
which, on reflection, the composer and his librettists
agreed to cut out. The wayward, impetuous heroine
is not, indeed, the sort of young lady whom one can
fancy singing scenas in set form with introductory
recitative, andante and cabaletta. Minnie Hauck
enters into the spirit of the character, lives it, and
never is anything else but " Carmen " from " Carmen's " entry until her tragic end; and it was
in a great measure to her performance that the
success of this very Spanish, very Bohemian work
was in the first instance due.

Minnie Hauck is the wife of the Chevalier Hesse
von Wartegg, known by some very interesting
works on Tunis and Algeria and other countries.

That versatile artist, Madame Marie Roze, has
also distinguished herself during the last few years
in the part of " Carmen." Of course she brings for-

ward the gentle side of the character. " Carmen "
has something of the playfulness of the cat, something also of the ferocity of the tigress ; and the
ferocious side of " Carmen's " disposition could not
find a sympathetic exponent in Madame Marie Roze.

    Carmen is known to be the latest operatic work
of George Bizet, who died at Paris in 1875, at the
age of thirty-seven—that fatal limit which neither
Mozart nor Mendelssohn nor Herold was destined
to pass, and which neither Schubert nor Bellini
reached by several years ; a limit, too, which marked
the close of Rossini's career as an operatic composer, for Rossini was just thirty-seven when
Guillaume Tell, his latest dramatic work, was
brought out—now nearly sixty years ago. Bizet was
not only the favourite pupil, but also the son-in-law
of Halévy, by whom he was regarded as a composer
of great promise. He was certainly a musician of
marked originality and brilliant fancy. Bizet
had just undertaken the composition of *Carmen*
when Mdme. Marie Roze, at the Opéra Comique,
obtained her first success in the *Premier jour de
Bonheur,* the last work contributed by Auber to the
stage which he had enriched with so many masterpieces. Bizet, attracted by Mdme. (then Mdlle.)
Roze's great talents, both as a singer and as an
actress, wrote the principal part in his opera specially
for her. In 1874, when the work was nearly com-

pleted, Bizet, accompanied by Meilhac and Halévy, the authors of the libretto, called upon Mdlle. Marie Roze to hear any suggestions she might have to make before the work went to press. The only objection she raised was based on the character of the heroine as depicted in Prosper Mérimée's tale. The authors, however, represented to her that it would depend upon the artist representing "Carmen" to make that personage very much what she chose. On consideration Mdlle. Roze consented to create the part, and her engagement in England alone prevented her from carrying out her promise.

Then Bizet, in order to secure the production of his opera without delay, rewrote the part of "Carmen" for Mdme. Galli-Marié, whose voice with its limited range has neither the low notes of the contralto nor the high notes of the soprano. Such notes, however, as she has at her command are of telling quality ; and both as a singer of expressive music and as an actress she is quite admirable. Yet, when *Carmen* was produced at the Opéra Comique, with Mdme. Galli-Marié in the part of the heroine, and with M. Lhérie as "Don José," the work did not please—a result which was explained at the time by two causes : first, that Mdme. Galli-Marié made "Carmen" too repulsive (an absurd statement, since Madame Galli-Marié even now is the most fascinating " Carmen " imaginable) ; secondly, that the music given to " Carmen " afforded no opportunity for brilliant vocalization, which, for the rest, would have been beyond Mdme. Galli-Marié's means. According to the original plan, as worked out for Mdlle. Marie Roze, " Carmen " was to be represented as capable of remorse ; and after the scene in which she foretells her death by the cards, was to be left alone, to give vent to her feelings in a pathetic air. Two fully developed airs were, in fact, written for " Carmen," which have never been heard : one in the mountain scene with the situation just referred to, and one in the last act, in the place now filled by the ballet music borrowed chiefly from the composer's *Jolie Fille de Perth*.

The part of " Carmen," as it now stands, has been objected to by two very distinguished prime donne who had been asked to appear in it : Mdme. Adelina Patti, who was present on the occasion of Bizet's opera being played for the first time at Her Majesty's Theatre, and Mdme. Nilsson, who had entertained the idea of impersonating " Carmen " some time beforehand, but could not reconcile herself to the character of the heroine. Mdme. Patti, however, declined to undertake the part, not from any uncalled for fastidiousness in regard to character, but because " Carmen " had a succession of little songs to sing, without one regular scena. Had she been acquainted with the work in its original form, with the two scenas written for Mdlle. Roze, she would possibly have accepted the part, in which she could not have failed to achieve brilliant success.

" Carmen," in which so many vocalists have been strikingly successful, is, strangely enough, the only part in which Madame Patti, when she at last undertook it, made no very favourable impression : apparently from too great a desire on her part to be original.

The first plan of *Carmen* has indeed been departed from in many respects, apart from the character of the leading personage. The bull-fight, according to the original design of the authors, was to be shown in the form of a tableau, occupying all the back of the stage; with live chorus-singers and " supers " in the front of the picture, and painted figures behind them. " Escamillo " was to have been seen triumphing over the figure of the fallen bull, while the crowd of spectators overlooking the arena shouted vociferously the air of the Toreador. In a dark foreground (the back of the stage being alone illuminated) the figures of " Carmen " and " Don José " were to be seen. As the work is now represented the bull-fight is abundantly suggested by the procession which precedes it and by the singing, the shouting, and the clanging of brass instruments which accompany it during its supposed progress. But the drama takes place only in the front of the stage between "Carmen" and her justly indignant lover; and this termination is more dramatic than the one first decided on. In the United States, however, the stage arrangement which exhibits the bull-fight in full activity is preferred, the passionate dialogue between " Don José" and his " Carmen adorata "—whom he adores so much that he will not suffer her to live for any one but himself—being still, we must imagine, preserved in its integrity.

Madame Marie Roze is the wife of the able and energetic impresario, Colonel Henry Mapleson, son of Colonel J. H. Mapleson, for so many years lessee and manager of Her Majesty's Theatre.

Mdlle. Alwina Valleria, the last-comer among those prime donne who have made a considerable mark in England, appeared for the first time at a London Theatre in 1877, when she fulfilled an engagement at Drury Lane, where Italian Opera was then being carried on under the direction of Mr. Mapleson. From 1877 until now Mdlle. Valleria has (with the exception of a visit to the United States in 1880) remained constantly in England; and as for several years past she has sung in English opera and oratorio, one feels an irresistible inclination to claim her, in spite of her American origin, as an English vocalist. Another ground on which such a claim might be based is the fact that she received her musical education at our Royal Academy. Of her own free will, moreover, she constituted herself an English subject when, not many years ago, she became the wife of Mr. Percy Hutchinson, of Husband's Bosworth, Leicestershire.

Alwina Valleria was born at Baltimore, in the United States. Coming at an early age to England, she entered the Royal Academy of Music, and there studied the pianoforte, taking up singing only as her "second study." After a time it was pointed out to her by Sir Julius Benedict that the order of her studies ought to be reversed; and now, without neglecting the pianoforte, she devoted herself more particularly to singing. There is no comparison, indeed, between the success to be obtained by a pianist and by a vocalist of equal merit. For one person who can appreciate good pianoforte playing there are a hundred whom good singing will affect.

Alwina Valleria's first success as a vocalist was gained at the Academy; where, after she had re-modelled her course of study, she carried off the Westmoreland prize for singing. After leaving the Academy she placed herself under Signor Arditi, with a view to the operatic stage; and she sang for the first time in public at a concert given by her eminent professor. Her success as a concert singer was immediate and complete, though it was not until later that, on the lyrical stage, her greatest triumphs were to be gained. Her first operatic engagement was at St. Petersburg, where Signor Arditi had accepted the musical direction of the Italian Theatre, and her first part that of " Linda " in Donizetti's well-known work. From Russia Mdlle. Valleria travelled south to Italy; and at the most famous of Italian Opera-houses, the Scala of Milan, sang leading parts for three seasons in succession.

In 1877, as already mentioned, Mdlle. Valleria joined Mr. Mapleson's company, of which Drury Lane was at that time the head-quarters; and in 1879 she appeared at the Royal Italian Opera, Covent Garden. Then she visited her native country, where she produced a deep impression as " Marguerite " in Gounod's *Faust;* so much so that she was obliged to postpone her return to London, undertaking meanwhile, with many other parts, those of " Margherita " and of " Helena " in Boito's *Mefistofele,* and of " Marguerite " in Berlioz's *Damnation de Faust.* Remarkably enough, Mdlle. Valleria sang the three parts of " Margaret," according to Gounod, according to Boito, and according to Berlioz, in the same week; and each different impersonation gained for her the most enthusiastic applause.

Returning to England in 1882, Mdlle. Valleria was engaged by Mr. Sims Reeves for the first of his farewell tours; and in the year following she became a member of the excellent English company organized and directed by Mr. Carl Rosa. "It was a lucky day," says an esteemed writer in the *Musical World,* "for Madame Valleria, and a luckier still for Mr. Carl Rosa, when she left the foreign for the national institution and devoted herself to English opera. Here the resources of her nature found their full scope, and it was here also that she was enabled to develop that 'special feature' to which allusion has been made at the beginning of this notice."

When Mr. Carl Rosa abandons the provinces and settles down in London with a theatre of his own, as before long he must do, the "leading lady" in his permanent opera company will, beyond doubt, be Madame Valleria.

One of the first prime donne of our time, Gabrielle Krauss, has, strangely enough, never sung in England. Until recently she was the principal dramatic soprano at the Paris Opera-house; and those who have never seen her will be glad to make her acquaintance through her portrait.

CHAPTER IX.

THE comic style in music has for many years past
been out of fashion. With the brilliant exception of
Adelina Patti, not one prima donna of the present
day has ever been seen in a comic part. It may be
said that *The Marriage of Figaro* is a comic opera,
and that in this admirable work Nilsson, Albani,
Lucca, and Titiens have all sung. *The Marriage of
Figaro* is, however, in its operatic form, a musical
comedy of rather a serious kind; infinitely more
serious, for instance, than Rossini's *Barber of Seville*,
though Beaumarchais' *Barbier de Séville* and his *Folle
Journée*, otherwise *Mariage de Figaro*, are written
in precisely the same lively and satirical style.

Adelina Patti is, in any case, the only great prima
donna of our time who has appeared in works of a
truly comic type; as "Rosina" in the *Barber of*

Seville, as " Norina" in *Don Pasquale*, and as the cobbler's wife in *Crispino e la Comare*.

In former days the Italians, inventors of opera, and also inventors of pantomime, used sometimes to confound the two styles; and Pergolesi and Paisiello, like Rossini in his early days—the days of *L'Italiano in Algieri*, of *Il Turco in Italia*, of *Il Barbiere*, and of *La Cenerentola*—wished not only to charm but also to amuse. Donizetti, more serious than Rossini (though in his serious operas he sometimes shows himself rather light minded), has composed one graceful work in the light comic style, *L'Elisir d' Amore*; and (to speak only of those that have remained popular) one very diverting work in the semi-buffo style, *Don Pasquale*. Even *Don Pasquale* is relieved from the monotony of perpetual drollery by a few semi-sentimental airs, and by the delightful scene of the serenade. But it is all the same a near approach to the buffo style of former days.

Bellini wrote no comic opera; neither did Verdi, with the significant exception of one which he attempted in his youth and which failed.

To show how completely the comic style in music has passed not only out of fashion, but out of credit, it may be mentioned that M. Ambroise Thomas, who began his career as a composer of light operas and of ballet music, brought an action after the production of his ponderous *Hamlet* in order to restrain a

manager from reviving one of his light operas—
"youthful sins," as he now considered them.

The comic spirit expelled from opera took refuge
in operetta. Seeing how dull opera had become,
Offenbach, whose first ambition it was to compose
serious music, and who, at the Théâtre Français,
where he was musical conductor, wrote interludes
and choruses for M. Ponsard's *Ulysse,* rushed in
where wise or at least serious men feared to tread.
Finding the field of musical comedy without an
occupant, he took possession of it, and therein dis-
ported himself in such a manner as to bring the
style into disrepute.

To trace the history of the comic style in dramatic
music we must go back to the early buffo operas of
Italy and to its pantomimes, which, as before suggested, were sometimes set to music.

Two noble Italian families, the Colonnas and Pan-
taleones, were made to furnish types of the wily and
of the witless buffoon, and both clown and pantaloon
may still be recognized in Donizetti's *Dr. Malatesta*
and *Don Pasquale.* If these analogies be accepted so
also must those which undoubtedly exist between
the "Ernesto" of the opera in question and harle-
quin, between the "Norina" and columbine.

The Italian opera-buffa found its way into France
towards the end of the eighteenth century, but did
not take root there. In Italy, as already shown, it

gradually gave place everywhere to serious opera; Rossini producing but few comic operas, Donizetti fewer still, Bellini and Verdi none.

The old Italian buffo style was marked by gaiety, without any suggestion of impropriety; and if the subject was sometimes frivolous the treatment was artistic. Opéra bouffe, however, as introduced by Offenbach, is generally objectionable, both on artistic and on moral grounds; and in the hands of some of Offenbach's imitators it has become notorious alike for frivolity and indecency.

It was not, indeed, until Offenbach died that his merit, as compared with the demerits of his successors, became apparent; and in Offenbach France, and indeed all Europe, lost not indeed one of its greatest but certainly one of its liveliest composers.

Having once convinced himself that he had no vocation for serious music, Offenbach affected anxiety not to be confounded with the graver masters of his art. On one occasion he is reported to have stopped the leader of the orchestra who, at an interval during a rehearsal, was playing passages from Mendelssohn's famous violin concerto, on the ground that the artist might, in a moment of forgetfulness, bring forward his reminiscences at the public performance; in which case, said Offenbach, "the public would think the music was mine."

To an expectant biographer (who is perhaps even

now at work on a " life "), he replied, in answer to
an inquiry as to whether Bonn was not his birthplace, that it was not he but Beethoven who had first
seen the light at Bonn.   These characteristic sallies,
however, were not outbursts of cynicism, far less of
vanity; they were simply ebullitions of fun.   Offenbach knew the great composers well enough to be
aware that he was not one of them.   He had studied
them, and in the early part of his career had himself
written serious music for a play whose claims to be
regarded as " serious " are not at all likely to be disputed.   In those days Jacques Offenbach was conductor of the orchestra and director of the music
at the Théâtre Français, and when M. Ponsard was
preparing to bring out his *Ulysse* it fell to the lot of
Offenbach to compose for the new work some inci-
dental pieces and a series of choruses.   The illustrious Meyerbeer had, in the first instance, been
asked to supply M. Ponsard's drama with the requi-
site musical pieces, and it had even been announced
in the journals, if not in the programmes of the
theatre, that the music would be from his pen.
Perhaps this aroused Offenbach, who possessed a
remarkable sense of humour, to imitate Meyerbeer's melodic phrases, his harmonies, and, above all,
the peculiarities of his orchestration ; or it may have
been that, without any idea whatever of fun, he
deliberately composed the music for *Ulysse* after
the manner of Meyerbeer.

The composer of *Le Postillion de Lonjumeau, Le Châlet,* and other entertaining little works, without having failed as a musician, had become a musical critic ; and in the *feuilleton* of *L'Assemblée Nationale* he wrote a long and interesting article on the music furnished by Offenbach for M. Ponsard's Hellenic drama : only he complimented warmly not Offenbach, but Meyerbeer on the work.

This mistake, made not by a mere critic, but by a composer of recognized ability, was undoubtedly an honour for Offenbach; and it may possibly have been this confounding of Meyerbeer with himself which made Offenbach at a later period take such pains to dissociate himself from two other German masters who had little indeed in common with him.

In the days of *Ulysse* and the Théâtre Français, Offenbach, besides being a composer and a conductor, was a violoncellist; and he cultivated his by no means trivial instrument with remarkable success. His portraits of this time represent him with a look of spirituality in his Paganini-like face; with a look also of grotesqueness, but with a distinct air of gravity such as in a violoncellist could not be thought otherwise than becoming. At the period of his collaboration with M. Ponsard he had evidently no idea of becoming the musical partner of Meilhac and Halévy, the future authors of *La Grande Du-*

chesse, La Belle Hélène, and of a long series of
so-called opéras bouffes, some of which, notwithstanding the frivolity of the style, have acquired a truly historical reputation. *The Grand
Duchess of Gerolstein,* for instance, belongs so
thoroughly to the period of the Paris International
Exhibition of 1867 that no adequate account of the
latter could be written without some mention of the
former.

The Czar of Russia and the King of Prussia (as
the now German Emperor was then called) went
both of them to see *The Grand Duchess;* and while
the Prussian Sovereign may well have asked himself
from what petty German State Gerolstein, with its
narrow frontiers and its diminutive army, was copied,
the Emperor Alexander had probably an uneasy idea
that the very despotic, but in her private relations
only too amiable Princess might be intended, so far
at least as her temperament was concerned, as an
imitation of his great-grandmother, the Empress
Catherine.

Bismarck, then but a Count, and Moltke, only
a Freiherr and a Lieutenant-General, went, like
their royal master, to see the great piece of the
day; and Baron Stoepel, the military *attaché* to the
French Embassy at Berlin, has told us in his celebrated reports how pleased Moltke was with everything he saw in Paris, including, it may be, the

performance of *The Grand Duchess,* with Mdlle. Schneider in the part of the heroine.

When Prince Gortschakoff, on his way to Paris, telegraphed from Tauroggen, on the Prussian frontier, to secure a box at the Variétés for the representation of *La Grande Duchesse,* political gossips declared that, beneath a pretended desire to witness the performance of a somewhat free musical farce, His Excellency concealed deep political designs. Europe afterwards learned that the venerable but light-hearted Chancellor of the Russian Empire was just as likely to make politics a cloak for amusements as to make amusements a cover for diplomatic intrigues; and there can be no doubt but that Prince Gortschakoff was as anxious as everyone else to see the great piece of the moment at the earliest possible opportunity. Even those who, in that *annus mirabilis,* did not reach Paris in time for *La Grande Duchesse* were not left altogether in the cold; for they, at least, got there early enough to see *La Belle Hélène,* by which it was followed, with Mdlle. Schneider once more as the heroine and M. Dupuis once more as the hero.

A good many critics have asked whether such a thing as comic music can really exist; and whether the mood of Jessica, who was " never merry when she heard sweet music," is not a general one. The question is easier to put than to answer. It is certain, meanwhile, that with *Don Pasquale*, produced just forty-five years ago, comic opera came to an end, to be replaced, rather more than thirty years ago, by Offenbach with opéra bouffe. The difficulty of arriving at any absolute decision as to whether or not there is a recognizable comic principle in music arises from the closeness and completeness with which, in all effective comic operas, words and music are mixed together. A good many competent critics would, undoubtedly, say that in its grotesqueness Offenbach's music, without avoiding the incorrect, borders at times on the vulgar. One may, in any case, affirm that it was always spirited, often ingenious, and at times really subtle. In his earlier works he dealt in all sorts of extravagant effects, and it was sometimes impossible not to be amused by his burlesque orchestration, in which instruments were joined together which most composers in their sober senses would have preferred to keep asunder, and in which passages suitable for one kind of instrument were for that very reason assigned to some instrument of quite another character. Offenbach's love of parody made him introduce, with a few necessary exaggerations, whole phrases borrowed from the composer whom he had undertaken to travesty. After a time, however, he abandoned imitations and burlesque effects and kept to the style which he had himself invented, and in which it cannot be said that he has any true successor. This alone would establish the fact that Offenbach in his way—a small way no doubt—was a genius. He possessed originality, and he could do something which no one else could do like him, or as well as he. "Mon verre n'est pas grand," he might have said with Alfred de Musset, "mais je bois dans mon verre." His glasses, too, were sufficiently numerous, and there was evidence of power in his very productiveness.

Finally, like other composers, he owed much to his singers, and, to compare with genuine musical art the art of being grotesque in music, Schneider was to Offenbach what Colbran was to Rossini.

CHAPTER X.

THE PRIMA DONNA AND SOME OPERATIC CONVENTIONS.

UNLESS she happens to be playing in one of Wagner's operas (though why they alone should be treated seriously it would be hard to say) a prima donna on our Italian stage, in imitation of the French actresses who originated the custom, reappears at the end of every scene which happens to have procured for her marked approbation. In the German Court Theatres this practice is absolutely forbidden, as is also the repetition of any particular piece in response to an *encore*.

Hisses a prima donna has rarely if ever to encounter; though hissed without just cause she would perhaps have a right to imitate the conduct of Mrs. Farrel, an English actress of the last century, who, dying in the character of " Zaria " in the *Mourning Bride*, and finding that the audience did not like her manner of expiring, rose from the

dead, and advancing towards the foot-lights expressed her regret at not having merited the
applause of the spectators. She explained, moreover, that she had only accepted the part to oblige
a friend, and hoped she might be excused for not
playing it better. This behaviour was absurd; but
scarely more so than that of a prima donna who
at one moment leaves the stage in a heart-broken
condition, and the moment afterwards returns full
of smiles to thank the audience for having applauded
her.

Playing in an opera, the action of which belongs
to a past century, the prima donna ought scarcely
to wear a dress of the latest fashion. This she
always does in *La Traviata;* the period of which
was put back by the composer precisely that the
personages of the drama might not be seen in the
garb of the present day. It need scarcely be said
that each character should appear in the costume
of the country and period to which the piece
belongs ; yet, whatever the male performers may be
wearing, the prima donna, superior to all considerations of time and place, shows herself in the dress—
probably in several dresses—of the present time and
of Worth's make. She does so not only in *La
Traviata,* but also in *Il Trovatore,* in *Les Huguenots,*
and many other works. Indeed, I can scarcely think
of one opera in which the prima donna does not

attire herself like a lady of the very year, and, by
preference, the very month in which the representation takes place.

The conventions admitted in operas are much
more remarkable even than those which are
recognized as indispensable in the spoken drama.
In the ancient theatre, as in the French theatre
of comparatively modern times, the scene of
every piece was laid in a public place. The personages came and went freely and naturally enough,
and it was not necessary to account for their
presence by the supposition of visits paid or
received. The strange spectacle, on the other
hand, was witnessed of people discussing private
and important affairs in an open thoroughfare, and
it so happened that no one ever crossed the public
place who was not somehow mixed up with the
intrigue of the play. The most natural of all
dramas, so far, at least, as regards stage presentation, was, until quite recently, that of England; for
our dramatists changed the scene as often as the
action seemed to demand, so that everything might
be said or done in its most appropriate place.

It was worrying, however, and sometimes confus-
ing to be shifted every five minutes or so to some
new locality; and of late years, under the influence of the French stage, it has become the
custom (except in melodramas recognized as such)

to confine every act to a single scene. A set scene may be thus secured as perfect as scenic art and stage upholstery can make it ; such a scene as can be prepared during the interval of an *entr'acte*, but which could not well be built up at the back of another scene while the performance was going on. There are dramatists, moreover, who, apart from the question of scenery and decorations, think it more artistic to tell the story of each act in a single scene; and, rightly or wrongly, it is the fashion just now to construct dramas and comedies on this principle. The principle in question may be regarded as a return to one of the famous "three unities," which can be all observed with advantage in cases where the subject lends itself to such treatment. But "unity of place," in connection with each particular act, though it may, and generally does, make the action of the piece much clearer, involves at the same time a considerable number of inconsistencies and even absurdities which actors and spectators seem by a tacit understanding to have agreed to overlook.

A German writer, who has recently published an interesting work on " The Conventional Falsehoods of our Civilization," has not condescended to deal with our dramatic conventions, many of which are as false as well can be. Under the one-scene-to-one-act arrangement, for instance, the stage represents, we will suppose, a room in someone's house. The house may be the mansion of a very rich man. The room will be used all the same by a great variety of persons for a great variety of purposes ; and it will have certainly three, probably five, and, it may be, as many as seven doors. A room with five doors (two on each side and one at the back) is the commonest thing on the stage, and in a room with less than three doors it would really be very difficult to carry out any sort of dramatic intrigue. In real life a room has rarely more than one door through which visitors and servants, master and mistress enter alike—no matter whether they are coming from the street or from some other part of the house. A stage room has generally a door at back (or, in theatrical parlance, "centre") leading to the street, and a certain number of side doors leading to different sets of apartments. Occasionally, too, this remarkable room has a door leading to the street by a passage not generally used. "Is there no other way out ?" asks some personage who had been on the point of leaving the house by the very door through which some other personage, whom he must not meet, was about to come in ; and a suitable exit—"exit in case of emergency"—is at once pointed out to him.

Again, in the modern "interior" corresponding to

the ancient public place, the inmates of the house, the visitors (whether staying in the house or not), the tradespeople, and any mysterious stranger whom it may be necessary to introduce, are all shown into the same room.   Or, rather, they enter the room of their own accord, for it is not customary on the stage, as in real life, to have visitors and strangers shown in by servants ; and very tedious it would be if these and other particulars of the realities of life were too closely followed.   Stage servants, unless mixed up with the intrigue of the piece, have indeed very little to do.   They are not, in a general way, expected to announce visitors; and a visitor will sometimes volunteer to do their work for them. " Here is a letter for you," says a character in more than one of M. Sardou's plays to another character ; " I took it from the servant who was bringing it up to you ; " or, " a messenger delivered it just as I was coming in."   The dramatist's justification in regard to these little improbabilities is that by omitting details wherever they are not absolutely indispensable he makes the action of the piece swifter and stronger.   Allow him a little license and he will produce a greater effect.   Sometimes when the large common room is full of people two of them find it necessary to exchange confidential communications.   In such a case do they go into another room as they infallibly would in ordinary life?

Not at all, for this would involve a change of scene. They simply say that they wish to be alone when the other personages leave them; but only to return as soon as the confidential communications have been made.

Trial scenes, so effective when properly handled, present difficulties not of place but of time. In domestic scenes the audience cannot be taken all over the house; first to the drawing-room, then to the dining-room, now to the mistress's boudoir, and now, again, to the master's study. Whatever business may be going on, whether connected with love, money, or murder, it must all be transacted in the same room, the proprietor of the place having apparently no other; and, in like manner, however long a trial would last in reality it must be represented on the stage as occupying not more than some fraction of an hour. Even if only a small portion of the proceedings be represented they must be strangely abridged; and in introducing in a murder case a speech for the defence one well-known dramatist, as if to avoid the inconvenience of bringing in towards the close of the piece a new character in the shape of a barrister, has made the prisoner defend himself. He knew, of course, as well as any of his critics that this was not in accordance with the practice of our criminal courts. He was working, however, not as a lawyer, but as a dramatist. It was above all things necessary for him to keep his leading character in a prominent position, and he must have felt certain that if the scene really interested the public no complaint would be made as to its being unreal. Everything in a drama is sufficiently probable if it can be made to appear so.

Operatic conventions include the conventions of the spoken drama as well as those peculiar to the drama not spoken but sung. An operatic " interior," for example, has just as many doors as any other stage " interior; " and people come in and go out as freely in a musical as in a purely dramatic piece. But Opera is reproached as unnatural even by those who accept the ordinary conventions of the stage. Not only, it is said, do personages in Opera sing when in real life they would speak, but they sometimes sing when in real life they would go away. " Now, as my danger's imminent, I'll sing," says a character in a burlesque; and at first sight there is doubtless something strange in such a proceeding. But in the spoken drama a character, before taking flight or rushing off to attack an enemy, will frequently deliver himself of a rapid soliloquy; and here we have the exact analogy of the song indulged in by the man who ought, realistically speaking, to be in such a hurry to depart that instead of singing about his going he would go at once. That the personages of a drama should make their utterances in the singing voice is only a degree more unnatural than that they should do so in rhyme or in rhythmical blank verse. One mode of delivery is just as much opposed to custom, if not nature, as the other. The declamation of trivial phrases in portentous music has, of course, a ridiculous effect; but this also has its counterpart in the rhymed comedies and dramas of France, which often contain commonplace thoughts expressed in the most sonorous language. Not that in representation this causes such a shock as might be expected. The audience soon get accustomed to the verse, as in Opera to the music, and accept it without criticism or inquiry.

St. Evrémond in France, and Addison in England, said, soon after the introduction of Opera from Italy, all that could be fairly said against it; and Addison's attacks were directed not against Opera in general, but against Opera played in the Italian language before English audiences. First he satirised the absurd practice that for a time prevailed of playing operas half in English, half in Italian. When it was afterwards arranged to give the whole representation in Italian he observed that the people had evidently got tired of understanding only half of what was said, and preferred that it should all be unintelligible. Then, speculating as to what future ages would think of so strange a fashion, he imagined posterity lost in wonderment at the notion of Italian having been so perfectly and so generally understood in England during the eighteenth century that our dramatic performances were habitually given in that tongue. On another occasion he suggested that the audience must sometimes be troubled with suspicions as to whether the Italians in their unknown language were not abusing them and calling them names. But against Opera as a dramatic form he had nothing to say. He indeed so fully accepted it that he wrote an opera himself; and Addison's *Rosamond* libretto is as full of operatic conventions as any other work of the same kind.

Many of the supposed defects of Opera are really the source of its greatest beauties. In the spoken drama verisimilitude is so far studied that the personages are only made to speak one at a time; but in an opera two, three, four, and sometimes as many as six and seven raise their voices all together. It is not in every opera that sestets and septets occur. But in all operas we meet with choruses in which crowds of people are heard shouting as one man. This is unnatural and contrary to everyone's experience. In real life several people do not speak at the same time unless they happen to be quarrelling; and, in any case, speaking at the same time

they would not be understood. Fortunately, however, combinations of voices are tolerated in Opera by
a very ancient convention ; and without it composers
would be deprived of one of their most powerful
means of dramatic effect. Many persons believe
that Wagner, from love of realism, set his face
against concerted music. This, in a systematic way,
he never did, for concerted music is to be found in
all his operas. He did not, after the manner of
most other composers, prepare situations with the
deliberate view of introducing concerted pieces.
Nor did he write concerted pieces simply in order
to show how ingeniously he could treat the voices.
He allowed himself to be guided only by the
dramatic requirements of his subject; and thus
it happened that in some of his operas no concerted piece seemed to be wanted. If, however, he
was inclined to dispense with some operatic conventions which by previous composers had been
generally received and acted upon (often, it must
be admitted, with admirable results), he introduced
conventions of his own, or, at least, pushed accepted
conventions to novel lengths. When, for instance,
in *Tristan und Isolde*, the king, suddenly entering at
the back of the stage, finds that he has been
betrayed, he takes no immediate action, but walks
to the front and there delivers himself of an agitated
soliloquy, leaving the lovers meanwhile to them-

selves. This is another case of " Now, as my danger's imminent, I'll sing ; " and the strangeness of the proceeding is scarcely lessened by the singing's taking a declamatory form. Again, the interminable address of the dying " Tristan " to his servant is a flagrant abuse of a convention which Donizetti has been ridiculed for turning to account in connection with the mortally wounded " Edgardo."

The operatic convention by which an expiring personage may sing and continue singing for some considerable time is no more remarkable, singing being once admitted as a medium of expression, than the analogous one, which, in the spoken drama, permits all the heroes and heroines of tragedy to declaim before they die. To those who refuse to accept the essential conditions of operatic art, almost everything that takes place in a musical drama must seem ridiculous. In all forms of art there are certain inevitable postulates ; and for lyrico-dramatic purposes it must be taken for granted that singing is as natural to man as speaking. Wagner, in one of the most striking passages of his " Opera and Drama," seriously maintains that men sang before they spoke ; or, at least, uttered cries of emotion before they learned to express their wants in detail and with precision. As a matter of fact, the children of the present day begin their utterances not by singing, but by shrieking. It is difficult, however, to say where one kind of cry ends and another begins; and if the original language of man is not song, neither is it verse, nor the epigrammatic prose of well-written comedy. Once, on the other hand, allow song as a stage language, and the tones of passion may be reproduced with all the intensity and force that music can give, and we acquire a form of drama through which much larger audiences can be effectively addressed than through the spoken drama—in which an assembly, a body of troops, or any crowd can join with voices and not with gesture only in the action of the piece, and in which various persons can, without perplexing the audience, utter either similar or diverse sentiments at the same time.

Unfortunately there are only too many conventions in Opera which arise not out of the very nature of the dramatic form, but only from the folly of librettists and composers. All the most hackneyed situations from the ordinary Drama have been imported into Opera; which must have been strongly felt by the critic who, asked why he disliked Opera, contented himself with defining it as " an entertainment in which a tenor, betrayed by a baritone, calls out, ' I love you ' to a soprano, who exclaims to the baritone, ' Do not kill him, I love him in return ! ' "

Mr. Carlyle, when he once made a visit to the Opera, disposed of operatic conventions in very summary style. "Music," he wrote, "has, for a long time past, been avowedly mad, divorced from sense and fact; and runs about now as an open Bedlamite, for a good many generations back, bragging that she has nothing to do with sense and fact, but with fiction and delirium only; and stares, with unaffected amazement, not able to suppress an elegant blast of witty laughter, at my suggesting the odd fact to her. Of the Haymarket Opera my account in fine is this: Lustres, candelabra, painting, gilding at discretion; a hall as of the Caliph Alraschid, or him that commanded the slaves of the lamp—a hall as if fitted up by the genii regardless of expense. Upholstery and the outlay of human capital could do no more. Artists, too, as they are called, have been got together from the ends of the world, regardless likewise of expense, to do dancing and singing, some of them even genuine in their craft. One singer in particular, called Colletti, or some such name, seemed to me by the cast of his face, by the tones of his voice, by his general bearing, as far as I could read it, to be a man of deep and ardent sensibilities, of delicate intention, great sympathies, originally an almost poetic soul, or a man of genius, as we call it, stamped by nature as capable of far other work than squalling here like a blind Samson to make the Philistines sport. Nay, all of them had aptitudes, perhaps of a distinguished kind, and must, by their own and other people's labour, have got a training equal or superior in toilsomeness, earnest assiduity and patient travail, to what breeds men to the most arduous trades. I speak not of kings, grandees, or the like show figures; but few soldiers, judges, men-of-letters can have had such pains taken with them. The very ballet girls, with their muslin saucers round them, were perhaps little short of miraculous, whirling and spinning there in strange mad vortexes, and then suddenly fixing themselves motionless, each upon her left or right great toe, with the other leg stretched out at an angle of ninety degrees, as if there had been suddenly pricked into the floor by one of their points, a pair, or rather a multitudinous cohort of mad, restlessly jumping, and clipping scissors, and so bidden there rest, with opened blades, and stand still, in the devil's name! A truly notable motion—marvellous, almost miraculous, were not the people there so used to it; motion peculiar to the opera; perhaps the ugliest, and surely one of the most difficult ever taught a female in this world. Nature abhors it; but art does at least admit it to border on the impossible. One little Cerito, or Taglioni the Second, that night when I was there, went bounding from the floor as if she had been made of indiarubber, or filled with hydrogen gas, and contrived by positive levity to bolt

through the ceiling; perhaps neither Semiramis nor
Catherine had bred herself so carefully. Such
talent, and such martyrdom of training, gathered
from the four winds, was now here to do its feat
and be paid for it—regardless of expense indeed.
The purse of Fortunatus seemed to have opened
itself, and the divers cost of musical sound and
rhythmic motion was welcomed with an explosion
of all the magnificences which the other arts, fine
and coarse, could achieve. For you are to think of
some Rossini or Bellini in the rear of it, too, to say
nothing of the Stanfields, and hosts of scene-
painters, machinists, engineers, and enterprisers;
fit to have taken Gibraltar, written the history of
England, or reduced Ireland into industrial regi-
ments, had they so set their minds to it. Alas!
and of all these notable or noticeable human talents,
and excellent perseverances, and energies, backed
by mountains of wealth, and led by the divine art
of music and rhythm, vouchsafed by Heaven to
them and us, what was to be the issue here this
evening? An hour's amusement, not amusing
either, but wearisome and dreary, to a high-dizened
select populace of male and female persons, who
seemed to me not worth much amusing. Could
any one have pealed into their hearts one true
thought, and glimpse of self-vision! High-dizened,
most expensive persons, aristocracy so called, or

best of the world, beware, beware what proofs you
are giving here of betterness and bestness.   And
then the salutary pang of conscience in reply.   ' A
select populace with money in its purse, and drilled
a little by the posture-maker : Good Heavens ! if
that were what, here and everywhere in " God's
creation," I am.   And a world all dying, because I
am, and show myself to be, and to have long been,
even that.   John, the carriage—the carriage, swift !
Let me go home in silence, to reflection, perhaps to
sackcloth and ashes ! '   This, and not amusement,
would have profited these persons.   Amusement, at
any rate, they did not get from Euterpe and Mel-
pomene.   These two Muses, sent for regardless of
expense, I could see were but the vehicle of a kind
of service, which I judged to be Paphian rather.
Young beauties of both sexes used their opera-
glasses, you could notice, not entirely for looking at
the stage.   And, it must be owned, the light in this
explosion of all the upholsteries, and the human
fine arts and coarse, was magical, and made your
fair one an Armida, if you liked her better so.   Nay,
certain old improper females (of quality) in their
rouge and jewels, even these looked some reminis-
cence of enchantment, and I saw this and the other
lean domestic dandy, with icy smile on his old worn
face, this and the other Marquis Singedelomme,
Prince Mahogany, or the like foreign dignitary,

tripping into the boxes of said females, grinning there awhile, with dyed moustachios, and Macassar oil graciosity, and then tripping out again; and, in fact, I perceived that Colletti and Cerito, and the rhythmic arts were a mere accompaniment here. Wonderful to see, and sad if you had eyes. Do but think of it. Cleopatra threw pearls into her drink, in mere waste, which was reckoned foolish of her. But here had the modern aristocracy of men brought the divinest of its arts, heavenly music itself, and piling all the upholsteries and ingenuities that other human art could do, had lighted them into a bonfire to illuminate an hour's flirtation of Singedelomme, Mahogany, and these improper persons. Never in nature had I seen such waste before. Oh! Colletti, you whose inborn melody, once of kindred, as I judged, to 'the melodies eternal,' might have valiantly weeded out this and the other false thing from the ways of men, and made a bit of God's creation more melodious—they have purchased you away from that, chained you to the wheel of Prince Mahogany's chariot, and here you make sport for a Macassar Singedelomme and his improper females past the prime of life. Wretched, spiritual nigger, oh! if you had some genius, and were not a mere born nigger, with appetite for pumpkin, should you have entered such a lot? I lament for you beyond all other expenses.

Other expenses are light; you are the Cleopatra's pearl that should not have been flung into Mahogany's claret cup. And Rossini, too, and Mozart, and Bellini, oh Heavens! when I think that music, too, is condemned to be mad, and to burn herself to this end on such a funeral pile, your celestial Opera-house grows dark and infernal to me."

CHAPTER XI.

Opera is objected to by two great classes of persons, those who think it unnatural that men and women should throughout a drama be made to sing—as if it were not equally unnatural that in tragedies they should be made to talk in blank verse, or even in rhyme—and those who do not care for music at all. Both these classes, however, entertain a sort of admiration for the operatic prima donna, who, unlike the work she adorns, seems to appeal to all sections of the community. Musicians and the sterner class of musical critics have never ceased to utter lamentations and protests in connection with the undue regard shown for the prima donna—often to the neglect, it must be admitted, of the opera in which she appears. To many the story will be familiar of the gentleman who, after taking stalls at the Covent Garden for the next Patti night, went back to the office to ask what opera would be played! From the time of Adriana Baroni, whose charms were celebrated by Milton in no less than three Latin poems, to the present day, when the star of the moment prefers to be praised in intelligible English, the prima donna has often been the cause of operatic success. For that excellent reason the position of the prima donna is one that excites much admiration, and some envy.

To be thoroughly successful a prima donna should possess a variety of gifts and acquirements in addition to perfect vocalization. She ought to be personally interesting, and the enthusiasm of an audience will be more easily aroused if to her artistic accomplishments she unites great personal beauty. Of course she must be an excellent actress, and it is absolutely necessary that she should exhibit the most refined taste in the matter of dress. To enjoy European favour she must have several languages at her command. Italian, if not the first, is the second language of every prima donna; and the most successful of contemporary prime donne have, like Malibran, the most striking type of the class, possessed a complete mastery of several tongues. Perhaps the gift of language and the gift of song go to a certain extent together. At any rate, examples, including some brilliant ones, could be cited at the present time, and close at hand, in

which the highest faculty for musical language
and a very high faculty for speech are combined.

When the time comes for examining the prima
donna scientifically, after the manner of Mr. Galton,
it will be interesting and important to note the
origin of the great prime donne (or prima donnas,
since the name has been received into the English
language) who, during the past and present century,
have from time to time enchanted Europe. They
have for the most part displayed aristocratic qualities, they have often been received into the aristocratic class, and in many cases have ended by forming part of it. But none of them have been of
aristocratic birth, and what is far more remarkable
is the fact that to very few of them does musical
talent seem to have come by inheritance. Scarcely
one has inherited her high artistic qualities from
her immediate progenitors.

The public have but little idea of the indomitable
energy that a great prima donna should possess—
called upon, as she is during the season (and with
a great prima donna changing perpetually from
capital to capital it is always and everywhere
the season), to take part in morning rehearsals,
afternoon concerts, evening representations, and
often private concerts when the operatic representations are at an end; or of the knowledge of
society of various kinds and countries which a

prima donna of the highest class cannot, with such a varied life, fail to acquire. She ends by knowing something of the artistic, literary, and fashionable society of every capital in Europe, and has been on speaking as well as singing terms with the members of all the principal Courts. The cosmopolitanism of the really absolute *prima donna assoluta* is one of the most remarkable things about her. Of the thousands of singers who dream of competing, of the hundreds who actually compete for the highest honours in the profession, of the dozens who are very near attaining these honours, there are scarcely more than three or four at any time by whom they are really gained; and from these fortunate few a certificate of nationality is the last thing that would be demanded. They may come from Italy, Canada, the United States or Sweden, from Hamburg, Paris, or Pesth. The one thing necessary is that, possessing the rare qualifications I have spoken of, they shall sing habitually in the Italian language. They are more than cosmopolitan, for instead of being citizens of the world—that is to say of no city in particular—they are citizens of each and every city at which they happen to be engaged.

Madame Patti independently of her operatic performances sings "Home, Sweet Home" in London, "Solovei" in St. Petersburg, "Si vous n'avez rien à me dire" in Paris. Madame Nilsson, without counting her Swedish melodies, has sung operatic music in Italian at Her Majesty's Theatre, operatic music in French at the Académie of Paris, oratorio music in English at our provincial Festivals.

Prime donne do certainly receive immense salaries. Still it must not be forgotten that their expenses—above all, travelling expenses and outlay for dress—are very great. They are for the most part charitable even to excess. They are surrounded at the theatre by attendants of all kinds, some of whom expect money for the most trifling services. Their addresses are known to all begging-letter writers, and when one of the principal mendicants of the metropolis fell some years ago into the hands of the police it is a fact that the name of a celebrated German prima donna, the late Mdlle. Titiens, was found at the head of the list of his probable benefactors. Then think of the number of occasions on which they are asked to sing gratuitously, and in many cases consent to do so! "It is so little trouble for her to sing," is the argument. But it is still less trouble for a millionaire to write a cheque; in spite of which the rich financier is but rarely so ready with a draft for a large amount as the prima donna of high repute is with her easily convertible notes.

Nevertheless, after making due allowance for the

prima donna's inevitable expenditure, the fact remains that she is exceedingly well paid. Indeed, no women receive larger incomes except Empresses and Queens. There is this difference, however: that the income of the Sovereign, apart from revolutions, is for life, while that of the prima donna is only for the life of her voice, which in the case of a happily constituted and exceptionally successful prima donna may be reckoned at twenty-five years— say from twenty to forty-five. A duration of twenty years for voice and of twelve for popularity would, however, be nearer the average. Among men no Minister of State is nearly so well paid as a prima donna. The salary of a first-rate prima donna may amount to double that of the best-paid Ambassador (say £24,000 a year), and she retains the right, denied to the Ambassador, of receiving presents.

Those who judge of the worth of others by what they conceive to be their own personal value are of course shocked to find that our most popular prime donne are so munificently rewarded. It is clear, moreover, that a priest, a professor, or a judge exercises much more important functions than the greatest of prime donne; only, being less rare, and their services less eagerly sought after by the rich multitude, they receive more slender remuneration.

It is not, however, the rarity alone; it is the rarity combined with the absolute excellence of the prima donna in which her attractiveness lies. Any *lusus naturæ* is rare. But Nature is not in a freakish, she is in a smiling mood when she creates the perfect prima donna, who may be called, not *lusus,* but *risus naturæ.* When it was stated many years ago at the Court of Bankruptcy what amount of salary was paid to a celebrated first soprano at the Royal Italian Opera, the learned Commissioner exclaimed that that was " twice the salary of a puisne Judge ; " and nearly a century before that the Empress Catherine, when she heard what terms Gabrielli demanded, replied that not one of her Field. Marshals received as much. Thereupon Gabrielli recommended the Empress to get her Marshals to sing for her. It would be difficult to say which would cut the queerest figure on the operatic stage—a Russian Field Marshal or an English Judge.

The truth is that the prima donna, though largely and often profoundly adored, has not yet been sufficiently studied, certainly not in that calm spirit of investigation which it is necessary but very difficult to bring to the contemplation of so charming a subject. From star worship to astronomy would be a great step, but if the nature of the operatic star were thoroughly understood its distinctive attributes would doubtless prove to be of a higher kind than passing devotees usually imagine. The prima donna was never more highly appreciated than in the present day. Like all persons who hold exalted positions, she is exposed to reverses, and a fall in her case amounts often to a catastrophe. Many prime donne have had tragic ends; and this may in some measure console envious persons who cannot forgive them their dazzling successes. Voltaire, or rather a character in one of Voltaire's tales, said of theatrical queens and of the style in which they were treated towards the end of the eighteenth century, " On les adore quand elles sont belles, et on les jette à la voirie quand elles sont mortes." We treat them with more respect in these days, and justly so ; for of many of them it may be fairly said that they are ornaments of society as well as of the stage.

As a rule they do not marry well. What agreeable woman ever did in the opinion of her male friends ? But the prima donna's husband deserves a separate study.

It is perhaps at her benefit that the prima donna is seen in her greatest glory. It is a horticultural as well as a musical *fête,* and systematic efforts are made to render each prima donna's benefit the greatest possible success from a floral as well as a lyrical point of view. If opera-goers generally would adopt such a mode of voting, the number of bouquets thrown to a prima donna would be a fair test not, perhaps, of her merit, but certainly of her popularity. It would say to the eye what applause now says to the ear; and the precise number of admirers belonging to one artist could be computed arithmetically. It would be desirable, however, that this form of suffrage should be universal. No one should be allowed to enter the opera-house without a bouquet, which, by an extension of edicts actually in force, might be proclaimed as an essential part of evening dress. Scrutiny, too, should be permitted, and care should be taken to prevent the unprincipled from throwing several bouquets in succession after the manner of those American electors who, in compliance with requests from their favourite candidates, "vote early and vote often." Other precautionary measures of more practical importance ought to be taken, or we may have our prime donne blinded and stunned by their rough supporters in front of the curtain; who at present hurl their bouquets with a force and precision of aim such as might be envied at Lord's, but is singularly out of place at the opera. Nerve is one of the essential requisites in a great prima donna, but it ought not to be tested by her ability to remain composed under a heavy fire of compactly made bouquets, not without stalks.

On these interesting occasions it will soon be necessary to regulate the enthusiasm of the public, and, perhaps, to introduce some such rules with respect to the throwing of bouquets as were proposed at the Brussels Conference in regard to warlike operations. Floral devices weighing more than half-a-hundredweight should be excluded from the list of projectiles that may be legitimately used, and orders might be issued enjoining subscribers and the public in general to hurl their missiles not at the head of the lady whom it is desired to honour, but at some point distant not less than six inches from the spot on which she may be standing. Should it be intended to drop heavy crowns on to the stage from a considerable height, warning should be given to the prima donna some seconds beforehand, so that she may have the opportunity of placing herself in some position of safety. Peaceable occupants of stalls taking no active part in the operations might be employed to pass bouquets from the boxes on the pit tier to the conductor of the orchestra, who would then hand them to the prima donna without injury to the lady or the flowers.

If some change is not shortly made in the custom of pelting the one or two leading prime donne of the day with bouquets and all kinds of floral devices, we shall hear at last of some popular vocalist meeting with the fate of the lady celebrated in

Roman history, on whom so many bracelets and other ornaments were thrown that she perished beneath their weight. Gold is heavier, no doubt, than flowers. But the bouquets hurled at a prima donna on the evening appointed for doing her homage frequently enclose jewellery, and instances have before now occurred of a fair benefit-taker being more than touched by the too solid compliment addressed to her.

The last appearance of the prima donna for the season is usually made either on the stage at her own benefit or in a box at the benefit of a rival, when she goes through a certain amount of dumb applause, or at the benefit of her rival's rival, when she applauds with genuine enthusiasm.

I like her best at her own benefit. There she is lyrical, expansive, sincere. The public is delighted with her, and she is delighted both with herself and with the public. It is interesting, however, to see her at the benefit of a rival, and to note how her seemingly energetic clapping of hands is attended by no sound. Even this visible but by no means audible demonstration of approval is not always indulged in when the object of so much carefully-guarded admiration happens not to be in a position to observe it.

" Giulietta, my love," I once heard a prima donna's mamma say to her somewhat thoughtless but perfectly natural daughter at the benefit of one of her rivals—a certain Mdlle. Chanterelle : " Giulietta, my love, Mdlle. Chanterelle is on the stage " (she had just been called before the curtain) " and you are not applauding ! "

" What is the use of applauding, mamma ? " replied the artless young thing, " she is not looking this way."

" No, my love," returned the mamma, " but her friends are."

Thus admonished, Giulietta began to applaud with much apparent violence. I warned her that if she did not control the expression of her ardour her gloves would suffer for it, but somehow they did not split.

At the benefit of the rival of a rival the prima donna renews, without, perhaps, being aware of it, the policy which in modern times has been especially associated with the Austrian Empire, but which is as old as the art of government itself. Giulietta dislikes Chanterelle heartily, because Chanterelle, who is engaged at an opposition theatre, is a light soprano, and is always trying to eclipse her in her best parts. Paulina, however, who appears at the same theatre as Chanterelle, and divides with her the admiration of the public, is a dramatic soprano, so that her success, however much it may vex Chanterelle, will not in the least degree disturb

Giulietta's peace of mind. On the contrary, every triumph gained by Paulina at Chanterelle's expense will fill Giulietta's heart with joy. Hence at Paulina's benefit she applauds without reserve, and without caring what happens to her gloves. But that it would spoil the effect of her toilet she would be ready to take them off and applaud with her naked hands. She at the same time urges her friends to throw bouquets to Paulina, and herself presents her with a wreath—does, in fact, all she can to strengthen Paulina, whom she does not fear, so as to weaken Chanterelle, whose increasing reputation sometimes alarms her.

All this is very sad. But the most adorable persons are sometimes slightly treacherous, and the prima donna in her dislike to rivalry resembles other artists. The great instrumental virtuoso can no more brook successful competition than can the eminent vocalist. I remember one distinguished specimen of the class—a pianist—telling me how he once went to the concert of a rival, and taking his seat in front of the audience applauded with enthusiasm all the most surprising passages in his rival's most astounding pieces. He did not, however, applaud the best executed passages, but only those in which he detected false notes. The pianist who applauded was the late Leopold de Meyer; the pianist who, according to Leopold de Meyer, played false notes was Anton Rubinstein; and that Rubinstein in his most frenzied moments does now and then make slips is well known.

What becomes of the prima donna's bouquets when they have once been thrown; when they have served their purpose, that is to say? Do they share the fate of Les neiges d'antan—"The snow of yester year?" "By no means; they can be thrown again," some cynic will perhaps reply. Indeed, at *café* concerts, music halls, and minor theatres of a low grade that may well happen. The prima donna, however, distributes hers among private friends who go to offer her their congratulations at the end of the performance; or, selecting two or three of the finest for herself, she leaves the remainder to her maid, who may possibly dispose of these perquisites to some enterprising florist. At a *café concert* to offer a singer a bouquet is only another way of presenting her with a few francs. The bouquet is handed to her, not thrown, and at the end of the concert is taken back at a reduction by the accommodating dealer from whom it has been purchased. But small things must not be compared with great, nor the doings of a singer at a *café* concert with those of an operatic prima donna.

When the last bouquet has been thrown, when the last rival has been feebly, and the last rival's

rival forcibly applauded, the prima donna prepares
to start on her travels. A prima donna who is
" not accustomed to travel" must be either very
young or can have met with no great success. The
truly successful prima donna, whose name a hundred
years hence will occupy a place in the history of her
art, knows the whole civilized world; London, Paris,
St. Petersburg, Vienna, Berlin, and Brussels, as
a matter of course; New York beyond a doubt;
and possibly she will have gone from New York
westward to San Francisco, or southward to New
Orleans. If diplomatists lived several centuries,
and could go on for two or three hundred years
without being placed in " disponsibility," a diplomatist would now and then see as much of the world
and of those Courts which, after all, form a very
important part of it, as a few celebrated prime
donne see now. Ambassadors, sooner or later,
publish their memoirs, but no prima donna has yet
published hers. Perhaps prime donne are less
observant than Ambassadors. It is their part, moreover, to give impressions rather than to receive
them. Otherwise a prima donna, in the course of
her career, is sure to come into contact not only
with the directors of all the great Opera-houses, but
also with the chiefs of all the great Governments of
the world. Indeed, more than one prima donna
might be mentioned who has conversed more

or less intimately with at least three or four Emperors.

"Which of them," I asked one day of a very distinguished prima donna, who enjoyed a large acquaintance among crowned heads, "which of them do you like best?"

"Well," she replied, with some hesitation, "the Emperor Alexander gives the best jewellery."

Another of more refinement selected Napoleon III., saying, "he is the most gentlemanly Emperor I know." ("C'est l'Empereur le plus comme il faut que je connais.")

The position of the prima donna, brilliant as it is, has for some time past been a source of great anxiety to some of her best friends. For her everything else is neglected, and managers are, with reason, warned not to place their trust too exclusively in the prima donna, lest some day they should find that by sacrificing the whole to a part—the prima donna's part— they have destroyed all interest in the opera as a consistent artistic work.

Without an agent or a husband a prima donna would never get on, and happy is the prima donna who can combine the two in one. As a rule, however, she requires the aid of two separate functionaries, one to attend to her business matters, the other to accompany her on her visits and excursions, and to direct her household. The husband will sometimes at the beginning of his career attempt to do the work of agent. But he has probably been accepted for ornament rather than for use, and his endeavours to save his wife the percentage levied by the musical middleman on her salary are not necessarily attended by advantageous results.

The ordinary agent is a man of business, which the prima donna's husband perhaps is not ; and by his superior acquaintance with the operatic market he is in a better position than the husband for knowing where the prima donna's services are likely to be required, and in what quarter they will, in a commercial sense, be most highly valued. Sometimes, no doubt, a prima donna's husband is a better hand at a scrittura than even the most practised agent. But such exceptions are rare. It is difficult, on the other hand, for the business agent to perform those higher agency duties which consist in judiciously nurturing and developing enthusiasm for the prima donna. The prima donna's husband, if worthy of the name, is really nothing more than an agent of a superior kind. But he is a diplomatic agent, not a commercial one.

The man destined by Fate or by Fortune to become the husband of a prima donna may love her for many reasons—for her beauty, her talent, her money, or for all these gifts and acquirements together. Sometimes she has a temper, which must

be taken into account.   But there is no reason for
supposing that, due allowance being made for little
caprices which a right-minded prima donna's husband
will be only too pleased to have the opportunity of
gratifying, her disposition is less charming than
that of other charming women whose lot it is to be
fed with perpetual flattery.   There are some women
to whom praise administered at fitting moments and
of good quality is positively beneficial.   It is like
water to an hydrangea.   Besides, the prima donna
may have an artistic ideal, keeping it constantly
before her without ever attaining it ; and in that case
the admiration lavished upon her will leave her unaffected by it.   It must be admitted, however, that
as a rule the prima donna is capable of taking in
any amount of adulation, and in the simplest, not
to say grossest, form.   A prima donna of the
third rank once asked a journalistic friend to
write something about her.   He excused himself on
the ground that he had never studied the vocal art,
and, worse still, had no technical vocabulary at his
command.

" Never mind that," she replied, " say that I sing
wonderfully well, and that no one could possibly
sing better.   That will be quite enough."

Now, the husband of this unaffected young
woman, who knew so well what she wanted, and
knowing it went straight to the point, would, if he

set any value on domestic peace and quiet, have been obliged by some means or other to get some such statement as the one on which she had set her heart placed publicly before the world. How would he set about it? If he understood his duty as a prima donna's husband he would have plenty of acquaintances on the Press. But there are some newspaper offices at which the proprietor is all-powerful, and others at which the editor will not allow the proprietor in any way to interfere with him. Then there are editors who refuse to dictate to their critics, and there are even critics who refuse to be dictated to.

The man who wields the pen is obviously, in the great majority of cases, the one to address; and the question then arises as to the best manner of addressing him. If the prima donna's husband is new to his business he will, perhaps, call himself. If he possesses a moderate amount of tact he will call with his wife; and there have been instances in which he has allowed his wife to call alone, he himself remaining outside concealed in the brougham. *Qui trompe-t-on ici?* one may ask with *Figaro* in the last case. The critic, without doubt.

Almost the first care of a prima donna's husband on arriving at a new capital should be to find out who are the most influential critics, which of them can with advantage be cultivated, and which, by reason of notorious surliness or some similar defect, had better be left alone. But the prima donna's husband who is well up to his work will find means to approach the critic, who piques himself on being inaccessible equally with the one who makes no effort to conceal his natural affability. There is danger even in a desire to be thought strong.

When the date of the prima donna's first performance has been fixed it will be for the husband to arrange about the bouquets, the wreaths, the garlands, and the recalls, the preparation of an address, the unhorsing of the carriage in which the prima donna had intended to drive home, and towards the end of the season the presentation of a set of diamonds on the part of the subscribers. These manifestations of delight must, of course, be varied according to the custom of the country in which the prima donna is singing, for what would in one land provoke enthusiasm might in another cause nothing but laughter.

A flight of doves, for instance, each dove bearing a streamer with a sonnet inscribed on it, might be very effective in Italy, but would not be appreciated in England. In Russia a prima donna is seldom after a great success recalled less than a dozen times; and the number amounts now and then to as many as twenty. This in England would be simply tiresome. Bouquets, however, may be thrown

at our Opera-houses in great profusion; and it is
for the prima donna's husband to see that the
supply is adequate to the occasion.

The custom of presenting a prima donna at the
end of the season with a set of diamonds is by no
means English ; and in London, where subscribers
to the Opera content themselves as a rule with ad-
miring operatic divinities at a distance, such testi-
monials could not very easily be got up. For farces
of this kind Russia is the classic land; and there
seems once to have been a period—before it had
been found necessary to emancipate the serfs, and,
in view of fresh loans, to publish the Budget—when
prime donne performing at St. Petersburg did
really bring away with them at the end of their
engagements a considerable amount of jewellery,
for which neither the prima donna herself nor the
prima donna's husband had been required to pay
one copeck. Times, however, are changed, and the
patrons of prime donne with them ; and the
bouquets offered to the prima donna at the St.
Petersburg Opera-house (they are not thrown, but
are passed from hand to hand until they reach the
conductor, by whom ultimately they are presented
in a direct manner) have now, as in other countries,
to be sprinkled with water and freshened up, so
that the night afterwards they may be offered again.
Nor are the gifts of jewellery made quite so freely

as of old. It may be doubted whether, without the assistance of the prima donna's husband, they would be made at all. It is on these occasions that the personage in question shows himself really invaluable. The season is drawing to a close. Again and again at each succeeding performance has the prima donna been summoned before the curtain. The students have called upon her, and begged her acceptance of an album in which they have inscribed their names : a genuine token of admiration this, though not, perhaps, intrinsically valuable. But the usual present of precious stones has not been made ; and, if only for the sake of the newspapers, the prima donna's husband has to see that it shall somehow or other be forthcoming. He has kept house well throughout the season. Not once has his charming wife had to tell him that the dinner was improperly served, or the drawing-room insufficiently lighted. He has asked the right people to her table, and has forgotten no presentable person who has ever rendered her the slightest service. But all this will avail him nothing if he allows her return to Paris or to London without a tiara of diamonds.

He has suggested a necklace, and he is not quite sure that he will even be able to manage a brooch and ear-rings. But she will be content with nothing less than a tiara ; and the worst of it is that it must be offered to her spontaneously as an homage to her talent on the part of numerous admirers.

However, the prima donna's husband knows how to entertain; and this has gained for him the reputation of being a good fellow. His conversation turns exclusively on the doings of his wife; but as the guests are all in love with her, the subject, however old, is for them always new. Often he has attached to himself a sort of toady and hanger-on, who at the same time plays the part of innocent lover to the wife. This mixture of courier and confidential friend can be counted upon for any sort of service; and on a particular evening, when the ladies have retired to the drawing-room and the prima donna's husband has gone to his own private apartment to get a brand of cigars which he can confidently recommend, the trusty dependent, the "friend of the house," rises and says that M. le Comte having fortunately left the room, the moment seems opportune for saying what he is sure is already on everyone's lips. How perfectly the Countess has been singing this season! What a charming woman she is! What a good fellow her husband is! Why not show their appreciation of his hospitality and her genius by presenting her with some diamonds? The proposition is received with acclamation. Prince Falutin puts his name down at once for a thousand roubles; General Nozoff follows him with a like sum; Count Monkievitch declares himself good for five hundred; and old Baron Donki cuts them all out by writing himself down for two thousand. When the husband at last returns—singing as he walks along the passage, so that he may take no one by surprise—a sufficient amount has already been subscribed, and it is no use his protesting; the thing is done.

Next day the jeweller has to be seen; and at an early hour he receives a visit from the prima donna's husband, accompanied by the faithful friend, Dourakoff by name, who, after setting the thing going, is determined to carry it through. The Count knows how to order jewellery, and the pattern having been chosen, he gives explicit instructions as to the execution of certain details, and arranges with the jeweller as to what it is all to cost. The jeweller has had dealings with Chamberlains and other high officials of the Court, and this has rendered him suspicious. He first made his money by buying at half their actual, and a twentieth part of their nominal, worth the diamond snuff-boxes presented by the Czar to persons whom he had deigned to honour, and afterwards reselling them for further presentation at twice their real value, and a fifth part of the value at which they would be charged to the Imperial Treasury.

" Who will pay for the tiara?" asks the jeweller.

" The gentlemen whose names you see on this list," replies the Count.

" Not Prince Falutin," observes the jeweller, " for his name is already on my books for a large sum, and I find it impossible to get the money; nor Baron Donki, for the old gentleman cannot pay what he has lost at cards; nor Count Monkievitch, who never comes to St. Petersburg except when his debts have forced him to quit some more interesting capital." When he sees the name of young Dourakoff, who has put himself down for a large amount, the dealer in precious stones tries not to laugh. Then, after running hastily through the list of names ending in " off," " ski," " vitch," and " in," he says to the prima donna's husband: " No, I am very sorry, but I really can't; unless, that is to say, you like to give me your acceptance for the entire amount."

" Of course!" responds the prima donna's husband.

" And you remember that the bill for last year's present of diamonds was never paid. Why not have them reset ? "

" They would be recognized; the St. Petersburg public is so clever."

At last it is arranged that the gift of the previous year shall be returned, and its value allowed in the bill for the new one; and on the occasion of the prima donna's benefit the diamond tiara is, amid general enthusiasm, presented to her on the stage in the name of Prince Falutin, Count Monkievitch, General Nozoff, Baron Donki, Captain Dourakoff, and the subscribers in general.

There have been examples of prima donna's husbands who had ended by persuading themselves that they could replace their wives at rehearsals, and who have not only paid visits in the prima donna's name, but have stopped at home to "receive" in lieu of her. One prima donna's husband is reported to have carried this species of infatuation so far as to offer to sit for his wife's portrait. But even the most modest of prima donna's husbands will, in speaking of his wife's engagements and performances, say "we" when he ought to say "she." "We have now thirty characters in our répertoire;" "we are getting up the part of 'Flora';" "we had a great success last night;" are phrases which are continually in the mouth of every prima donna's husband.

There are prima donna's husbands of a very different type from that which I have hitherto sought to depict; men who, instead of accepting their position and doing their best for their wives, live upon their earnings without making any effort towards increasing them, and too proud to perform the honourable duties of shawl-bearer, to which those who are not married to the prima donna so eagerly aspire, make a point of never being seen in public with her. Sometimes a prima donna's husband of this class loses his wife's money at the gambling table, or, under pretence of being a gambler, dissipates it in a manner still more reprehensible.

Sometimes the prima donna's singing-master, recognizing her talent beforehand, snaps her up before she has had an opportunity of displaying it in public. Or if she has escaped her singing-master the manager is probably lying in wait for her with an engagement not for a stipulated number of years, but for life.

The social position of a prima donna, as long as she remains single, extends over so much ground that it is really undefinable. Afterwards it is regulated to some extent by the status of her husband. Wherever she is invited he, of course, must be asked; and unless he be a man of tact he runs the risk of being looked upon as little better than the husband of a professional beauty. In view at once of her art and of her happiness, she cannot perhaps do better than marry a leading member of her own profession. No one can wish her to become the wife of some titled or untitled millionaire, who will be egotistical enough to withdraw her from the stage. Such a one is not a prima donna's husband: he is simply a man who has married a prima donna. But let us not blame him, nor, above all, envy him. Let us reflect rather that though it is not given to every man to have a prima donna for a wife, yet every man may, and ought to, make his wife his prima donna, and not only *prima,* but, moreover, *sola ed assoluta.*

THE END.

INDEX TO NAMES.

F.

G.

H.

I.

T.

V.

W.

Z.

INDEX TO OPERAS AND ORATORIOS.

A.

B.